Walking on
With Jesus

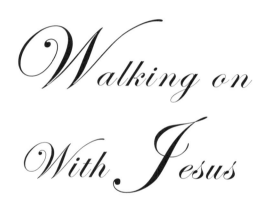

Walking on With Jesus

90-DAY DEVOTIONAL JOURNEY
FROM GOD'S HEART TO YOUR HEART

ROSALIE WILLIS STORMENT

DESTINY IMAGE™ EUROPE srl
Via Maiella, 1
66020 San Giovanni Teatino (Ch) – Italy

"Changing the world, one book at a time."

This book and all other Destiny Image™ Europe books are available at Christian bookstores and distributors worldwide.

To order products, or for any other correspondence:

DESTINY IMAGE™ EUROPE srl
Via Acquacorrente, 6
65123 - Pescara - Italy
Tel. +39 085 4716623 - Fax +39 085 9431270
E-mail: info@eurodestinyimage.com

Or reach us on the Internet: **www.eurodestinyimage.com**

ISBN: 978-88-89127-92-6

For Worldwide Distribution, Printed in the U.S.A.
1 2 3 4 5 6 7 8/13 12 11 10 09

Dedication

To all who long to know our Father God more intimately. That we, with faithfulness, vulnerability, and transparency, might allow Him free access to our hearts as we respond with trust, obedience, peace, love, and joy. That together we might continue to give Him greater access to speak to our hearts. That we, like Abraham, might be known as "God's friend" (James 2:23 AMP).

Table of Contents

Now It Begins

Go Forth With Praise and Thanksgiving

Time Is Your Friend

Destiny Proclaimed

Foreword

To know the Lord Jesus Christ as personal Lord and Savior is the foundation of our Christian experience. To fellowship with Him on a daily, moment-by-moment basis is a joy available to any child of God who chooses to make Him the center of living.

To give Him preeminence over all else opens the door to an intimate relationship. It is to choose His Presence first and foremost. Yes, it is a choice, a choice open to each of us. It is a choice Rosalie has made and maintained.

We all grew up knowing and loving the beautiful song "In the Garden." We enjoyed singing, "And He walks with me, and He talks with me, and He tells me I am His own." The message of those words was not challenged. It was a sweet thought, and the tune was pleasant to sing. We loved it, and still do. It was beautiful and made us feel good.

But for many of us, perhaps most of us, it was a lovely sentiment which was not embraced as a reality in our own lives. Otherwise, why should we be surprised or even skeptical when someone actually makes it a daily way of life? Rosalie has done this; and her writings reflect her journey as she has truly walked and talked with Him. She shares that journey with us through her books.

As you read, may you be inspired to seek His face, to grow in grace, and to be nurtured by a daily exposure to His Word and His presence. In the words of an unknown poet: *"Lord Jesus, make Thyself of me a living bright reality. More real, more intimately nigh than e'en the dearest earthly tie."*

As Brother Lawrence practiced our Lord's Presence working in the kitchen, just so we can do the same wherever we are and whatever else we may be doing. To whatever extent we do this, Rosalie's books and her example will be bearing fruit for eternity. There will be no regrets for time spent enjoying His Presence and worshiping at His feet. Everything else in life will take on new meaning. Burdens will be lighter, victories will come more easily, and darkness will be scattered at His feet.

Yes, walk on with Him. Live in His light and in His love until His image is stamped on your heart. When you walk with Jesus, you will never walk alone!

Frances J. Roberts, 1918-2009
Author, *Come Away My Beloved*

Preface

I was blessed to be raised in a godly home, knowing God as a loving, compassionate Father, a Father I loved with all my heart. But it wasn't until the early '70s when I became captivated by the Scripture *"pray without ceasing,"* that my life became wonderfully changed forever! I determined in my heart that I would include Him in every thought, word, and action, so that my life would be as a prayer. Shortly after I made that decision, I discovered that God was not only pleased by my decision, but He also wanted to speak to my heart. What a joy to learn that God actually created us for loving fellowship and longs to speak to us in return. That He didn't create prayer to be a one-way monologue, but a dialogue that we might come into intimate fellowship with Him.

There is nothing more exciting in life than walking with God, sitting in His Presence daily asking, "Father, what is on Your heart for me today? What is it that You want me to know?" Or, "Dear Father, how do I respond to this difficult situation?" He is always there to comfort, encourage, and to give wisdom and understanding.

Walking on With Jesus represents many years of writing down every precious word received and daily walking in loving, intimate relationship with Him. Each word He speaks is a treasure never to be forgotten; each word is to be enjoyed, learned from, and read over and over again. His words impart comfort, direction, wisdom, correction, strength, character, love, delight, grace, faith, hope, patience, healing, and life, causing us to become transparent reflections of His love, peace, and joy. Through it all He teaches us how to love His treasure—His people—as He does, with truth, faithfulness, forgiveness, and honor.

Introduction

My child. (*Yes, Lord.*) It shall be clear to you the path that you shall take, and the way will be bathed in light so that you shall not miss it, nor be distracted, nor sidetracked. The vision is strong and shall remain strong unto its fulfillment. Worry not nor be distraught, but know that what I have planned for you shall be, and you shall rejoice and be glad. Carry on with a song in your heart and determination to finish the way with honor. My blessings go with you, My child. The refreshing of mind, body, soul, and spirit shall come and buoy you up. Press onward! Press onward!

I will lead you into experiences that will have no road map of others' lives, so don't seek for the security of a road map. Learn to love and enjoy the beauty of a jagged crag, the beauty of unexplored territory. We shall strike forth an unmarked trail in the wilderness. You shall need My guidance for each step. Others shall follow to make it a well-marked trail, deeply imprinted across the wilderness. You shall be among this new breed of trailblazers, but a trailblazer must be disciplined. Accept the mantle of obedience. Let go of your own desires and inner cravings. Surefootedness is brought about through sustained patience. Surefooted you shall be. Let it not be said that you had not the fortitude to persevere, for persevere you shall, and we shall see it through to the very end.

Quiet your spirit before Me each day. I shall lead you into what must be done. Nothing shall be left unattended. Rejoice as each day builds upon another, for in that building comes strength, fortitude, and an elastic spirit. Growth is never easy, but is helped along with a quieted, peaceful, unperturbed spirit. Let Me quiet your spirit each day and prepare it for the events of the day to come. Then discuss each day with Me at the close of the day, and with each day we shall grow together. Now carry on with My peace within you.

Hold steady, straight, and sure. Blessings go to the one who holds a steady path in My direction. My light shines out to guide his every step. The blessings of My heart go forth to you today and you shall know the path that you shall take.

Love Is the Key

*You shall love the Lord your God
with all your heart, with all your soul,
and with all your strength*
(Deuteronomy 6:5).

Day 1

Soar forth! Soar forth! Readiness to do My will is the prerequisite for My perfect will to come forth. Be not afraid to step forth with confidence and soundness of step, for I shall guide you and lead you to know how you shall proceed. *Gradualness* is a virtue and is My leading for you. *Preparation* is the key to success. Bring forth your storehouse of knowledge as brought forth by Me. Be prepared! Be prepared to know My will at every turn. *Patience!* Patience too is a virtue to be pursued with quietness of spirit. *Confidence!* Confidence is My word to you this day. Look up and rejoice at every turn in the road. My way for you is steady plodding, step by step.

Believe this day all that I have lain before you to do and to be. Your work has been given you to do by Me, and I shall carry it through to the very end, every last jot and tittle. Release unto Me your fears for today and tomorrow. Nothing shall befall you that we cannot handle with distinction. All things work together for good to the praising, joyful, trusting spirit. Rejoice this day and be glad, for the foundation has been laid with soundness, and the structure of My love has been built exceedingly well.

My word to you this day is *Blessed Assurance!* It is yours, My child. Take it to yourself and treasure it. Reach forth with your heart and embrace it forevermore. This day shall be filled with sunshine. Worry not. The sorrowful shall be uplifted and the joyful shall go on their way with joy.

Steady yourself this day with sure footing securely planted. My leadings, to you, will be sure and strong. Vary not from the straight path and be agile and alert. Coupled with faith is determination. Listen to My words carefully. It is not the fly-by-night decisions that are lasting, but the day-by-day stick-to-it-tiveness that brings forth lasting fruit, the moment-by-moment determination to walk in what I have given you to walk in.

Roll with the tide this day. The rhythm will establish you and bring you into a quiet place. You will know My leadings to you, and you shall follow them. Fret not. Set your course with determination. You shall not waver.

Be established in Me. Be what I have called you to be. Look up and be confident and rejoice. Be secure in the knowledge of My care for you. Be removed from the problem, for with Me it is no problem. Be resourceful, for I have given you much and called you to much. I will continue to give you the desires of your heart. You shall not want for any good thing. Ascribe unto Me praise and thanksgiving. Together we shall move mountains.

Health is an elusive substance. You must hold onto it tenaciously, or it will flit away. You have been given the keys to health and prosperity. Hold on to them as if your life depends on them, for it does. Life can be lived two ways: with greed and foolishness or with dedication and commitment. Each reaps its own rewards: failure and disappointment or fulfillment and prosperity. The choice is continually yours to make. Fulfillment and joy are yours, My child, as long as you stick to your commitment to purity and truth.

Day 2

Blessed is the one who comes in the name of the Lord. His days shall be filled with sunshine and tears, but I am the abiding one. Nothing passes by Me unseen. Every detail is under My control. Be still and know that I am God of every circumstance. Regrets and anxieties are needless. Go forth each moment washed in the Blood of forgiveness and freedom, knowing My constant, watchful care.

My child. (*Yes, Lord.*) Listen to the rustling of the trees when the breezes blow. (*Why, Lord?*) It is their sighing against the pressure of the wind. They bend but they don't break. When the breezes stop blowing, they stand tall and erect with strength, knowing that when the wind blows once again, they will be prepared for the onslaught because they are flexible. (*What keeps them flexible, Lord?*) They don't take the pressure of the wind personally. They don't feel that the wind is out to get them. Stand watch on your heart to remain in a state of forgiveness.

Seek not acceptance for yourself, but give acceptance and reach out in love and compassion.

The seeds of wrath have grown and brought with them discord and unrest. Capture the seeds that they continue not to grow, for they would bring destruction and ruin. Love is the key. Give forth of My Spirit through love and forgiveness. Remember to smooth the way with concern and loving acceptance. You will see the walls come tumbling down and be pleased with the added blessings of harmony and a propensity of acceptance. Refrain from any sort of attempt to save face. That is not the issue at stake. Let your heart go out with love and acceptance. Let your words be words of tribute and acknowledgment of worth. Blessed are those who can lay down their right to acknowledgment to bring forth the acknowledgment of another.

Blessed are the merciful for they shall see God. Build not walls of protection but be vulnerable and transparent. Blessed are the peacemakers for they shall see God. Blessed are you when you suffer for My sake, for the blessings of My heart are yours. I have turned your mourning into joy, your sadness into thanksgiving, and given to you blessings evermore. Stand on the Rock of My Salvation. Forsake not your stance of joy and thanksgiving, for unto you have I poured out my wealth of blessings evermore. Fear not the dark, for it is bathed in light. Fear not the night, for it is followed by the bright dawn of My blessing. For unto those who seek My will, I have made manifest the wonders of My Kingdom. Nothing can deter them from their appointed walk with Me. Nothing can shatter, scatter, nor detract from the wholeness of the walk I have appointed for them to walk in.

Many times I have cradled you in My arms and comforted you. Many times have you looked to Me to rescue you and tenderly protect you. Know that I have not wavered from My promises to you. One by one they have found a place in your heart, and you have believed with an unfaltering belief. These are My gifts to you: strength in the midst of the storm, light in the midst of the dark, and hope that transcends all doubt. Surely My loving-kindness has led you and protected you. So now go forth unafraid, rejoicing in My might, for it is yours—perceiving, receiving, and committing all that you have and are into My loving care. I have brought you into the vast and unending knowledge of My love for you. Go forth with joy. Go forth with soundness and wholeness of heart, for I am with you.

Day 3

Fortitude in the line of fire. Stand strong, stand firm in love. Be unmoved from the course that I have given—to love with unfailing love by My Spirit, love brought forth by My Spirit and sustained by My Spirit. Walk with understanding, compassion, warmth, and commitment to those you love. Let your love be known. Receive from Me a double portion. Go forth determined to walk in My love, to give forth of my love. Left behind are the tares of self. You shall move forth with surety and strength, and we shall rejoice together.

Walk with a light, sure step. I have fashioned for you a pathway that you shall traverse with joy and thanksgiving. Blessed assurance is yours, My child, for I have given it to you. You shall know heart peace as few have known, heart rest that shall bring you joy. Listen with your whole heart. There is much I have to tell you, much for you to learn and know. The time is now. Open up your heart to receive. Abundant blessings go to the listening heart. No good thing shall be withheld from you. Respond with alacrity and delight and I shall respond to you with fullness of joy. Have you not heard? Have you not seen the rewards I have stored up for you? There is much to be done, much to experience and know. Seek My Kingdom and all these things shall be added unto you.

The words of My Spirit shall ring forth with a clarity that shall let you know the where and the when to move into action. Words alone do not convey the spirit of My love. Actions and words work together to bring freedom and the resolution to love. Lift up before Me others, that I might bestow upon them the reality of My love, that they might know that I Am that I Am. That I reside in hearts and not in cold stone walls. Bless them with a continual understanding of their vulnerability. Let them know that you love them on a human level. The spirit level will come later. Feed the soul before you feed the spirit. Blessed are the pure in heart for they shall know God's ways. Walk in honesty and walk in truth.

My child. (*Yes, Lord.*) Never resort to an outward show to gain affection and love. The outward show brings My indignation and wrath, for it is your feeble efforts as were Cain's to gain My acceptance on his terms instead of Mine. Do not perform, but be, knowing My love for you is constant and sure. Give forth of My love naturally, without striving, and it shall be returned to you tenfold. Think on this!

Gain strength of spirit by doing and giving forth of My Spirit liberally as I do lead. Give forth under My leadership and know My guiding hand. Rejoice in the now, My child. Rejoice in the fullness of Spirit I have given to you and let your fullness be known by My guiding hand. Rely on Me and you shall see My hand of blessing continue to fall upon you. The time of further rejoicing is drawing near just as the rider and horse draw near bearing good tidings. Bend your ear unto Me that we might walk in divine fellowship one with the other. Forsake not your diligence to hear and follow My Word to you.

Rely on Me

"Behold, God is my salvation,
I will trust and not be afraid;
'For Yah, the Lord,
is my strength and song;
He also has become
my salvation'"
(Isaiah 12:2).

Day 4

Break away from the stealthy infringement upon your time with Me, My time. Let your peace come from a word spoken in due season. Manifest your love for Me by the sacrifice of your time. You shall know the truth and the truth shall set you free. Set forth your determination to follow My Word. Pass on My Word to thee. Pass it on freely as I have given it to you. Pass it on without fear of reprisals. Let Me take what you have and multiply it.

Hang on to your dreams. Go forth with the promises ringing in your heart. Press forward to attain the prize. Leave behind all that encumbers and be buoyed up by My Spirit. Be one with My Spirit through trust and reliance. Move in trust. Have your very being steeped in trust of Me, loosed that I might do My will through you. Blessings abundant are yours.

Make a joyful noise unto the Lord your God. Serve Him with gladness. Let not the cares of this world shake you from your firm stance of unconditional trust. Let your yeas be yea and your nays be nay, knowing from whence cometh your answers. Break loose from that which binds you. Make a clean break from the moral decay that you see all around you. Break loose to come up higher unto Me. Relax into Me. Let your light shine. Do not dim it through ingesting the world's beliefs. Concentrate on Mine. That is the only way to become strong. Measure up to your walk by housecleaning your mind. All things that are clean and pure, think upon these things.

Plant the seed of forgiveness. The ground has been plowed. Now put the seed in and watch it grow and reap a harvest of love and eternal life for those you love. Plant the seed deep that it not be plucked from the garden but that the roots go down deep through sincerity and truth. Stay on neutral ground but plant your feet firmly. Blessed is the one who can loose the reserve of the other through pure motives and aspirations. Blessed art thou.

You shall know the truth and the truth shall set you free to "rejoice in the now." You can't truly rejoice in the now until you've made peace with your past. Loose yourself from the spirit of anxiety and know that wherever you go, I am there to love you and do you good. Rest in that knowledge. Let your heart go out to those whom you have depended upon for your sense of worth. The umbilical cord has been cut. Now when you reach out with love, you will not expect feeding back. You will not be disappointed when it does not come back to you. You will no longer turn to physical food for compensation. That has changed. Now you will look to Me for feeding, love, and acceptance, and reach out with the love you have received in return from Me. The cord is from Me to thee, not from them to thee! Bask in My love, My child. Let it warm you through and through.

Day 5

Lay down your defenses. Let them come to rest. (*What defenses, Lord?*) The defense of appearing, "worthy enough". Just be! Learn to appropriate My wholeness and rest in that wholeness. Respond to others with that same love and acceptance that has been poured out on you by Me. Plunge headlong into the joy of your salvation, lacking in nothing. Rejoice and be glad.

(*Father, what is Your word to me today?*) *Joy!* Let your joy be known, for I have filled your very being with the joy of My Spirit. My Spirit fills you and encompasses you to bring you forth into everlasting joy brought forth through faithfulness. Let your joy be known, My child, for it resides deep within you as a deep and flowing stream to be tapped at will. (*How do I tap it, Lord?*) *Praise!* Praise is the instrument of tapping into My joy! You shall see an ever-increasing manifestation of My joy in your life.

Remain steadfast and alert, ever ready to be a hearer and doer of My Word to you. Let not your heart be troubled, but step forth each day in the victory that I have prepared for you. Weary not in well-doing. Strike your colors and keep them flying through wind, rain, and sunshine. Strengthen your inner spirit with praise and thanksgiving. Enter in with abounding joy.

Straighten out your lifestyle. Bring forth the positive and shun the negative. Blessed art thou, My child, from beginning to end. Liken your walk with Me to a kangaroo child tucked in its mother's pouch being jostled up and down but protected and safe. Be on the alert! Let not the negative pop up to rob you of your peace. Walk in the positive. Reflect My love and peace.

Be still and know that I am God! Bask in the sure knowledge of My Spirit at work in you. Fetter out the good from the bad, the right from the wrong, the true from the untrue. Discern and know. Blessed is he who knows his Father's ways and follows them without deviation. His path shall be blessed. Know the difference between relinquishment and sanctification. Relinquishment is brought on by a desire to do My will. Sanctification comes forth through steadfast obedience to the relinquishment with joy. Let your joy be known. Accept and implement it into your life to bring forth the victory and joy you seek. Day by day, sanctify yourself before Me. Let your temperance and light shine forth as a beacon light of hope and transformation to those who reach out to you for hope. Thence they shall be led to Me.

Stretch out your arms to me as a winged bird in flight in submission to Me. Speak what is on your heart—your doubts, needs and feelings. Establish your ways. Meet your inadequacies head on. Speak them to Me that I might bring them to naught. Lean not unto your own understanding. Let Me enlighten your doubts and misdirected feelings. This is not possible through silence. You must bring them unto Me unadorned.

Weariness is not a thing of the flesh but of the heart. Worship Me for who I am, as well as for what I have done. I am Lord of lords, Creator of the universe, and I desire to be Lord of your life. Bring everything that touches you to Me and if you will obey what I show you to do, you will arise with Me, and our enemies will be scattered. My sheep hear My voice. They incline their ear unto My voice and are glad. Blessed is the one who hears, believes, and obeys.

Day 6

Be a transmitter of My love. Back not away from the needy of spirit. Respond with the balm of My love planted firmly within you. Great shall the harvest be. I shall bring unto you many who shall need a touch from Me by thought (prayer), word (encouragement), and deed. Continue to feed on Me that you might be a wellspring of living water, ready in season and out of season, to do My will and be a blessing to many whom I shall bring.

Trust not in humans. Put your trust in Me! Do not expect what they cannot give. Repent and go on. The wages of sin (bitterness) is death. Repentance brings life. Repent and rejoice in Me. Lighten your load as you go along. Carry not that which was not meant to be carried. Take it not to yourself. Repent for the immediate hurt and give it to Me. Then go on your way rejoicing. It is no fun to poke at someone who refuses to be hurt. When you turn on them with like responses, they are justified. That is why I say, love and turn the other cheek. Anger cannot feed on such an environment. It can feed upon itself but not upon you. Keep your spirit pure before Me. Do not give anger or bitterness a moment to breed.

Blessed art thou, My child. From the rising of the sun to the setting of the same, I will be glorified in your life. I reveal to My beloved ones My plans for them in advance that they might know the magnitude of My love for them. Step aside and let Me work in your life. To grasp the concept, rely on Me totally. Be not concerned with the details. See the overall picture that I have and will give you. Blessed is the one whose spirit sees beyond the natural into the world of My reality. Rely on what I show you and on My sight. It is a walk, not by natural sight but by supernatural might. Put your trust in Me forever. Remain at peace in your spirit. Remain at peace with My Spirit in you. Blessed and to be emulated is the one who can walk in this way. Be that one! Set your sails by the compass of My Spirit which encompasses round about you and is in you.

Release unto Me the fear of rebuke. Be free to speak as I shall give you to speak. Know the framework. Let Me fill the interior. Many shall come to know of My love for them in deeper ways, of My compassion for them, and of My delight in them. They shall see the strength and soundness with which I guide their lives and they shall know of My closeness to them with every breath they breathe. Remind them of these things along the way and leave not out the joy of this relationship with Me. Spread the Good News! My Spirit reigns in their lives to do them good, to bring them peace, to lighten their load and to lead them with perfection. Be My mouthpiece! Give forth the Good News!

Day 7

Continue on the course I have given you. The blind follow the blind, but you shall walk with your eyes wide open and drink in the glories of My Kingdom. Wrestle not with the whys and wherefores. Walk with Me day by day basking in My love for you. The whys and wherefores shall take care of themselves. Basic trust! It all boils down to basic trust. Do you trust Me in all things? If so, be at peace in all things.

Once again I say, struggle not with the whys or wherefores. Let Me take each moment and make of it a delight. Lighten more of the load from your shoulders as you lift each moment to Me for My touch, for your delight. Deliverance is release from bondage. Be released from the bondage of the pain of reproach and uncertainty. For unto you I have given the desires of My heart for you. Open your heart to receive with joy!

Your heart shall overflow with the goodness of My Spirit to you. Think not of past sorrows. Look to the immediate future with joy and anticipation. My heart reigns within your heart. (*Lord, this whole year has been difficult.*) Yes, but harken to the sound of birds singing. Make way for the promise of Spring. Listen, for I shall make of you a singing heart, a singing spring of living waters, bubbling up with joy and thanksgiving, giving forth of My Spirit. You shall see coming forth to you an abundance of blessings from My heart. Give ear and listen to the coming of My Spirit. You shall see it. You shall hear it, and you shall know from whence it comes. It comes from Me. Look for its coming. Stand forth in the radiance of My smile. I shall lift you up and speak through you words of life. Lift Me up, and I shall lift you up.

Receive Your Calling

*[God] has saved us and called us with a holy calling,
not according to our works, but according
to His own purpose and grace
which was given to us in Christ Jesus
before time began*
(2 Timothy 1:9).

Day 8

My blessings have been as a sprinkle, sprinkled as the blood of purification to make you a living sacrifice worthy of your calling. Now stand forth ready to receive your calling. Much has been in preparation. You have called upon Me, and I have answered your cry. Revealed from the beginning of time shall be My plan for you. Gird your loins with the strength of My Word. Don't let down the intensity of your search and desire to walk in the fullness of My Spirit. Let the weak and weary take the side roads. You take the main road, the shortest route but not the easiest, that My warriors take. Strengthen, strengthen, I say, by drawing on My strength, My wisdom, and My peace through My Word and My Spirit. You shall not know the disillusionment of defeat, but always the joy and delight of victory. It is yours, saith the Lord of Hosts. You shall see! You shall see! Tarry not as to the passing scene. Keep your eyes ever on the horizon of My love for you, ever on the big picture of My provision for you. Victory it is! Victory it shall be!

Do not let misgivings cause you to stray from your course. Remember My blessings, promises, and teachings. The Sprit of the Lord shall go before you and multiply your conquests and victories. Stick to the high road of My calling. Measure and weigh the results with My promises. You shall be pleased and lives shall be blessed.

The doors of My heart are open to you. I have prepared you, strengthened you, and made of you a fine warrior in My army. Now step forth with the banner of truth flying in the breeze. Realize your dream, your dream to be a blessing to many. Reach forth as I shall show you. As far as the eye can see, so shall you see My blessings for you and beyond. Your days are numbered for struggle and for blessing. Enter into the blessing of your Lord. Blessings untold I have for you. Your heart shall sing with joy. Let not your heart be troubled. Let your heart be raised up in the heavenlies, for there I am. Nothing can touch you there. Make of your heart a dwelling place of joy and peace. You shall see wonders untold that I have reserved for you.

Yours shall be a way led by Me. It has been brought forth by My hand. Night and day I have led and taught you by My Spirit. Forsake not the truths that I have taught you but hold them in reverence and let the light shine from them to light the paths of many. I shall overcome in all ways. Fear not for the words I shall give you to speak, for they shall bring life, healing, and freedom to and for many. Rely on My Spirit at all times. Let Me show you the direction to go. My light shall continually shine upon the way, and you shall know when to move out and when to stay your hand. My peace shall prevail. Together we shall prevail in victory!

Day 9

Struggle not with the whys and wherefores. I have been with you the whole way lighting your path with truth. Let that light shine now with brilliance. Straightforwardness is still a virtue. Nothing shall be lost, destroyed, or mislaid along the path, nor accepted that is not from Me. I have protected you, led you, and brought you to a wide place of blessing. Lest you say, "I am worthy," I have brought you through troubled and mired waters, and yet the mire has fallen away and left only My truth and blessing. Pride causes the mire to stick.

Maintain a quiet and alert spirit. Resist the desire to become agitated and unsure, for have I not led you and prepared the way for you these many days and years? The time will be there to accomplish all that I have laid before you to do. Be My ambassador of goodwill and quiet wisdom. Enter into this time with confidence and strength of purpose, the purpose of gaining knowledge. Leave the running around with agitation and frustration to those with less of My Presence within them. The race goes to those with steady persistence, not those who run with agitated spirits. Do not spurt and sputter. Flow steadily as I lead.

(*What kind of songs would you have me sing, Lord?*) Songs of praise and thanksgiving—songs that lift up the heart to rejoice, that lighten the load and make the heart sing. Yours is a ministry of reconciliation, bringing My children to joy and peace through praise and thanksgiving. Remain steadfast and unmoved, believing in My power to bring forth the promises in your life. Rest in My love.

Behold your God! Feed on My Word! Come to know the truths more profoundly. Base your every thought on the truths of My Word. Throughout history, I have led My people according to the amount of light they were willing to walk in. Obey My word to you. Make of your heart a habitation of peace. There can be no doubt that I have led you thus far. Let Me lead you on. Remain steadfast. How do you know My will? The heart knows. Spread your seeds of faith, love, thanksgiving, peace, and praise with confidence, for I am with you. You shall know peace like you have never known before. It is transferable. Go to it! Spread your wings; fly! Let them catch the wind currents to carry you far and wide to meet each destination of My choosing. Many shall there be, and great shall be the rejoicing of those who are touched.

Regard in your heart, take notice of and pay special attention to the times and the seasons of My visitations to you. First was the planting of the seed. Then was the tender care and nourishment of the seed and the joy over its growth. Next came the fruitfulness and joy that fruit brought. Then came the pruning and the elimination of contaminants. This period was grievous but necessary. A quiet season followed where the tree grew strength and fortitude for the storms of life, that it would stand tall and straight, unmoved. Whereas it could give fruit before, now it can also give shade, peace, comfort, and protection. If a tree is allowed to produce too much fruit, it ruins the tree, breaking limbs with the weight and destroying its beauty and its ability to give shade, peace, comfort, and protection. The tree must have seasons of quiet and unfruitfulness that it might draw in its strength, drawing on the Son and nourishment to grow full, strong, and beautiful. Enjoy this time of quietness and renewal that you might once more, in My time, give forth fruit, higher in quality and sweetness. Rejoice in the joy I have given and the pleasure of My company.

Day 10

Pleasing are My children to Me who walk in praise and thanksgiving, giving glory to My Name. The time has come to lean on My promises with tenacity. I shall not fail you. Stretch out your heart to receive the abundance of My love for you. You are blessed, now and forevermore. Trust in being My precious child is your song. Let Me orchestrate. You sing the song, and through that song My Spirit shall go forth. Hold fast to My promises. Faith grows as you trust. Resist the urge to panic. Be persuaded that I am able to keep that which has been committed unto Me against harm.

Refrain from comparisons. Judge not; compare not. Unsolicited advice brings anger. Sought-after advice and council bring blessing and delight. Blessed is the one who knows truth and knows when and when not to present it, that it be appreciated and not trampled.

To brush away a tear, to lend gentleness and strength is your calling. Be My messenger of love. Maintain a gentle, loving, peaceful, joyful spirit filled with thanksgiving, and we shall continue to prevail. Many blessings are missed when one tries to speed up My timetable. Consider the lilies, how they grow. They neither toil nor spin. They trust and behold My radiance with faces upturned.

Don't watch the passing scene. Tune into My love for you, an uninterrupted flow, undisturbed by circumstances. Tarry not over the hurt and rejection. Move on to the joy and security of My love. Reflect not! Move on! Let those who reject, reject. You accept all!

Hear My everlasting Word to you. Be persuaded of My love for you. Be brave and surrender your trust to Me. Let not your heart be troubled, neither let it be afraid, for I will continue to give you the desires of your heart, to strengthen you, to uphold you, to make your way straight. Blossom forth. Continue to grow in beauty and in strength. Maintain a quiet assurance of My love, for I shall lead you and guide you with gentleness and with care. Stand tall! Stand firm! Resolve to walk with Me!

Turn around and look at the fruit that has come forth in your life, the new branches that have sprung to life. New growth brings the need for more nourishment. Now is the time for that need to be met. Pursue that desire for the nourishment of My Word, that the new growth might continue to grow and bear fruit. Bring forth the desires of your heart day by day. I shall hear you and make you prosper.

Triumph, victory, and success, all words to express coming events. Burst into the sunshine of My love. Be a radiator of My love and the essence of My peace and joy. Be My ambassador of goodwill. Let My people know, "My God reigns and all is well with my soul." Put a watch on your soul day and night to rejoice in all things, for all things work together for good to those who love Me. So rejoice with trust and thanksgiving. Be a peace giver. Be that beacon that by its very light shows the way to salvation. Striving has ceased. My peace reigns! Rest in the peace of My love, and others shall rest in the peace of your love which is My love. Unto you I have given the ability to give. It shall be the joy of your being. Be all that I am. Give forth of My Spirit!

Day 11

Let Me hear your songs of joy that I might open the world to you. The days have moved quickly, each day bringing maturity and peace. Reliance on Me has been the key to success. Now move forward with continued reliance on Me, and together we shall move into new realms of service. I shall lead you and show you new avenues you thought not of. Stay grounded in My Word and let not up your stance of faith in Me. Many shall the opportunities be and great shall be the joy to your heart. Relax and let Me lead with surety and strength. Be not pressured nor grieved from lack of understanding. Simply rest in My provisions.

Stand firm. The elements cannot withstand one of Mine, try as they might. My protection is yours. Withstand the tricks of the enemy. Stand firm, unafraid. My love is upon you and round about you, keeping you steady. Fear not, for I am with you, giving strength of word, strength of purpose, and strength of love. Forming in you is the sound realization of the needs of My people. With that realization shall come the tools needed for action, to be the effective instrument of My peace. The blinders have been taken off that you might see the abundance of My Kingdom. Not by power, not by might, but by My Spirit saith the Lord. Joy everlasting is a gift. Maintain it in good health. Blessed is he who comes in the Name of the Lord. His horn shall be full to overflowing and nothing shall disturb his peace.

Many seasons have come and gone to bring you to this place, this place of fulfillment and need. As I have promised, each need shall be met, each promise fulfilled. Break loose and let the singing spill forth from your heart, the song of praise that is locked up there. (*I could see hundreds of singing birds bursting forth from my heart and flying forth with freedom.*) Sing every day with thanksgiving, joy, and gladness. Singing is your salvation, the door to your heart. Enter in with all your heart. Let it not be said that you did not enter in for lack of commitment. Let it be said that you persevered and prevailed. Now raise your voice in singing and in praise, for your God does reign. Sing Hallelujahs; sing Hosanna in the Highest. Let the freedom of your heart and joy ring true and vibrant for all to hear; and hear they shall, for I shall bring you to a wide place of My destiny for you and My Spirit shall rejoice with you.

Make of your heart a resting place. Come often to the well to be refreshed and refurbished, for the need shall be great. Maintain an unruffled spirit. I have said the desires of your heart are the desires of My heart for I put those desires there. Continue on, rejoicing on the way. Nothing shall deter your steps. I have spoken, and it is. Be assured, be sustained, and be confident of this very thing, that what I have begun, I shall complete. A storehouse of treasure have I placed in your heart. Continue to feed that storehouse with the treasure of My Word.

Sing to Me a new song of gladness brought forth from frustration, for the time of My visitation is upon you and all shall see the beauty of the Lord through you. Break away from the old and burst forth into the new. Be established in My love for I have established you in the mire and brought you forth onto dry land. Be strong in the might of My Word to you for I have taught you and brought to you wisdom and the ways of salvation and peace. Be My mouthpiece through the peace and song in your heart. The world shall see and hear that Jesus Christ is Lord! Stay close to My heart.

Day 12

Believe and know that I have been with you from the beginning. Let My Spirit reign within you. Tie down the loose ends that flail about through the application of My Word. Application of My Word is the key. Apply daily. Make mention of My Name often and know My Presence daily. Stand in the midst of the trial. Stand and refuse discouragement. Remain steady, alert and agile, unafraid and unperturbed, for I am there to light the way in the darkness and bring you forth into My light. Fear not for the future, for I am there. Fear not for the past, for I am there. Fear not for the present, for I am there. Live one day at a time by My Spirit. Be comforted, My child. I am with you!

Strength of understanding comes with time. Rush not headlong into the darkened place. With time, My wisdom shall come. Wisdom shall come as the night follows the day, and you shall follow that wisdom assuredly.

Listen well to My commands that balance out My blessings. Come into My Presence regularly. Continue to sit at My feet and learn. Be a communicator of My Word through thought, word, and deed. Stand tall in My Spirit, flanked on either side by the strength of My love. You shall inherit the blessings of My Kingdom in full measure, pressed down and running over. Be a processor of My Word, a developer. A developer takes the film that cannot be seen or understood and makes it into beautiful pictures that can both be seen and understood.

See and rejoice. Be not afraid to see and discern, for I am bringing a new day filled with new blessings and new ways. The old ways will not fulfill the needs of the new day. It is a time of change. Change brings upheaval, but it shall be followed by blessing. Maintain a quiet undergirding faith in My ability to move on your behalf. Beauty for ashes, a heart filled with love, has been My gift to you. Release it unto others.

Day 13

Release unto Me all worry and concern. Relinquish all hold upon your life unto Me, for I do care and I do all things well. You can rely on Me in all things. Be not afraid of the future. Look not to the past. It is a new day filled with the delights of My Kingdom. The door has swung wide. Enter in now! Relinquishment is the key to entering in. The times and the seasons have born fruit, the fruit of My constant and abiding love. Labor not to understand. Rest in My love. My love shall be a beacon light to you and shall lead you to vast and myriad places of My choosing. Release unto Me the details. Be at peace. All is in My hands. Contemplate the joy of My Salvation, of My leading and guiding hand. Contemplate My provisions for you and those you love. You shall be astounded and amazed at what I have in store for you. Rejoice and be glad. Let the rafters ring with praise and thanksgiving.

Now you shall see. Now you shall discern. Now you shall become part of the solution, part of the pattern of the cloth, the covering of My people. Struggle not to find your place. It shall come to you as the night follows the day. Let Me soften your contours, bringing you into alignment, and then send you out to be My representative of love and peace. Be a student of My love that you might pass it on.

Resist the temptation to flee. Stand your ground in the power of My might, not by your power or your might, but by My Spirit saith the Lord of hosts. Many shall be the opportunities to flee, but you shall not. You shall not, for I am with you, bringing victory and salvation. Stand your ground. Be My light in the darkened place. You shall rejoice in the fullness of My victory in you, through you, and for you. The stage has been set. All is in readiness.

Bask in the Warmth and Peace of My Love

The Lord is my shepherd;
I shall not want.
He makes me to lie down in green pastures;
He leads me beside the still waters.
He restores my soul
(Psalm 23:1-3).

Day 14

On eagle's wings you shall fly, buoyed up by My Spirit, recognizing and experiencing My perfect will in your life. Lie back and let the wind currents catch you in flight and carry you along My chosen path. Struggle not. Enjoy the peace that My Spirit gives. Bask in the warmth of My love. Be at peace, My child. Be not hurried nor grieved. Bear not the burden of coming events. Let Me sing through your being. Let Me be your spokesman. Let Me be the light through which you shine. Let Me carry the load. Let Me be the burden bearer. Wherever you go, whatever you do, My guiding hand is upon you.

Blessed are the ones whose trust is in the Lord. Their lives are like a bubbling brook, bouncing over rocks and debris, unencumbered, moving with the current with joy and total victory. You are blessed. Go with the flow this day. Bask in the Sonshine of My love.

Measure your progress by your peace. Be not in a rush to accomplish all that is set before you. Let the pieces fit together. Don't force them together. You shall see order and discipline descend and take up residence. Let time bring forth perfection in every way. The days are numbered and assigned. Take them one at a time with joy. Blessed assurance is yours that much is prepared and shall come forth. Rise above the seeming indecision and frustration. Rise above the negative aspects and let My Spirit reign once again in your heart and mind. Be still and know that I am God. I have led you beside still waters, and I will restore your soul. Enter into the multitude of joys I have for you. Let your spirit reign in the quietness of your soul. Back off from the hustle-bustle. Let quietness and peace be your joy. Among the many joys of My Kingdom is the ability to enjoy the quietness and peace that I give. Rest in My love. Quiet your spirit within you. Let the tranquility and beauty of My creation be a soothing, healing ointment to your soul.

Slow down the pace. Place your trust back into My hands. Peace shall descend and order shall come into being. Back off. Take a look as I see it. It is a time of reflection and strengthening, not one of building anew. Be content to be. Be content to simply see and soak in the splendor of My Kingdom. It is a time to grow strong. Bask in the Sonshine of My love. Let the rays penetrate into your inner being with their warmth and light. Let My peace bathe your inner being with joy. Maintain your stance of faith. I shall not let you down, and you shall know direction and protection. Let Me bring healing to your aching body, mind, and heart. It is a time of healing and renewed hope. Let the tranquility of this place be a balm to your spirit bringing healing and contentment. Take the time to enjoy!

Day 15

Strength, joy, and trust go hand in hand. Lift up your heart and rejoice. Let no sadness be found. Let the rafters ring with the magnitude and strength of your joy. Sing the songs of the Kingdom of God. It is a new day filled with the rich blessings of My Kingdom. Do you not know that you are a child of the King? Rejoice and sing! Let the rafters ring with your joy and laughter. Enter in with all your heart, and you shall know heart peace. Blessed is the one who comes in the Name of the Lord. Joy, gladness, and the strength of My Kingdom are your inheritance. Stamina will return and the grace to use it wisely. It is coming, a time of restoration and fulfillment.

Stand guard on your heart to keep it soft, flexible, and unembittered. Make of your heart a resting place for My love so that others might rest there too, as secure as they are in My love. Be a breath of fresh air, fragrant and sweet. Others shall find My love through yours.

Keep a stout heart, filled with love, wavered not by what you see and hear. Plant your heart deeply in My love and let it rest there unperturbed by the seeming passing scene. Peace, peace like a river, shall overcome your soul. Let it be a balm to your spirit, bringing with it a new dimension of love. Be a peace giver, born from My love to you. Be an instigator of My peace and joy.

Draw your sword. Cut the ties that make you weak. I have said, "Stand tall in My Spirit." I will draw those to you who need My touch.

You are free to be My ambassador of love, peace, and joy—all gifts of My Spirit. You have many times been unavailable. Now you shall be available for My use.

Study My Word with diligence. New treasures shall you find. New vistas of My love and care for you. New heights of understanding and discernment. Walk with diligence and might. Master the art of hearing and speaking My words. Listen, speak, and grow. The time has come to expand and grow, and grow you shall. Diligence becomes a way of life, once tasted and practiced. New zeal has entered your heart and shall continue to the glory of your Father. Be confident of this—I love you, and together we shall not fail!

Be not afraid to pour forth My Spirit upon My people who walk in loneliness, fear, confusion, and greed, and all the many and varied ways that are not of My Kingdom. Your life shall continue to be a watering spring, drawing many to Me. Be not afraid to proclaim My Word and My works, for they shall continue to bless you and sustain you. Be that channel of love and blessing to My hurting, wandering people. I have put within your heart a tenderness that My lambs can sense and feel. They shall be drawn to you, and through you they shall know My love. They shall drink and be satisfied. They shall seek and they shall find. I have prepared a banqueting table for them, and they shall eat and be satisfied. Many, many shall know of My love, and they shall see and believe. Hesitate not to respond with open arms. Tenderness and love shall be your strength. Steadfastness is the key, the key to all I have in store for you. The windows of Heaven are open wide. My blessings abound to you and nothing shall stop their appointed course to you.

Day 16

Rejoicing in the present lets My Spirit reign, for rejoicing relies on trust and faith which are the bulwarks of My peace. No wind of trial shall diminish you or knock you over. The tempest shall blow, but you shall remain firm and strong, able to withstand and remain steady. My word to you this day is, remain steadfast in My love. Wrap it around you as a cloak. Let Me handle the details. You handle the rejoicing.

Your spirit shall sing within you as you give forth of My Word to a hungry world. There is a hunger for My Word among My people, and you shall give forth of that Word in ever increasing amounts. Be not afraid of the outcome. Give forth and I shall bless. (*How do I begin, Lord?*) There will be a burning within your spirit to share what I have given you, and share you shall. It shall come forth as a water spigot, fresh, clear and sparkling, dancing with joy. Be a spokesman for My heart. Rise early and seek My face. Let it not be said that you give forth from an empty bucket. Let Me keep it full to overflowing. Rivers of living water shall come forth from you in ever-increasing amounts, and My heart shall sing, and your heart shall sing, and we shall rejoice and be glad together. I shall make of you a strong rock of My love and compassion.

The joy of the Lord is your strength and it shall continue to be so. Linger over and delight in the joys I bring your way as a child handles a beautiful jewel, turning it over and over in its hand, not trying to figure out its facets, but simply reveling in its timeless beauty, in the awe of its sparkle and life. Be a communicator of that sparkle and life. Its reflection shall shine forth to others, and they shall be warmed by the glow. Life grows in warmth. You shall reflect warmth to those who are new and warmth to draw new life and strength to the seasoned veterans. Now take it a step farther. My Word is that jewel that reflects the light, the glow. Be a reflector of that light as you continually look into it, turning it over and over in your hand, reflecting its warmth and life-giving glow. The Word, the Word, the Word! Your life is in the Word. And the life you pass on to others is from the reflection of that Word. Magnify the Word, rejoice in the Word, and reflect the Word!

Erect within your heart a sanctuary of praise. Let it be unto you a place of refreshing and peace, a place to draw apart and draw strength. Loose the restraints and go forward with strength of purpose and enthusiasm, and I shall bless you abundantly. Lay down your reluctance and strike forward to reach the mark, the zenith I have raised for you. I shall lead you gently and with care.

The strength of My Word never varies. It is like a metal stake poured into concrete, unmovable and unchangeable. Be at peace and rejoice, for My promises shall come forth unhindered, unhurried, and unyielding. You can set your heart on that. Blessings, blessings, blessings! You shall be blessed, you shall bless, and you shall bring forth blessings to others as yet untapped. Strength of purpose combined with strength of will, My will, brings forth victory. Be still and know that I am God. I bring forth strength and will of purpose.

Day 17

Unmarked trails are ahead, waiting for your footsteps, ready to reveal My truth. Rejoice in the present for it is Mine. Rejoice in the past for it has brought forth the present in all its glory. The future is Mine to bring forth as I will, but know that I love you and do all things well. Be assured that what I have planned is good and will come forth at its appointed time. Peace, My peace I give unto you. Not as the world gives peace, but peace solid and undisturbed by places, people, or things. Place your trust in Me, unmovable and unperturbed, for I shall bring you to a solid place of My making. Release unto Me your fears for the future.

Liken your life unto a beach ball. It bounds along where I take it with joy and trust, anticipation and exhilaration for what is next. Suddenly it punctures, and the air goes out of it. It is shocked; totally repairable by the Father, but vulnerable. (It was such a pretty ball—idolatry.) (Will it be pretty again—lack of faith.) (When will it be repaired—self-pity.) Receive again the bouncing ball that I might take it again where it pleases Me.

Stand in the awareness of My love and protection. Stand in the awareness of My fulfillment in your life. I shall not fail you. Be refreshed. Be revived, and be at peace. (It has been a beautiful day of refreshment, Lord.) It shall be ever thus. I have tucked into each day places of refreshment. Look, and you shall see and experience My refreshment on a continual basis.

Open wide your tent. It is a place of refreshment and rejuvenation and so shall it ever be. Rejoice and be glad in the task I have given you. Resentment and reluctance cause tiredness. I have given to you that you might give without reservation, freely and with joy. Take your rest when I give it without guilt. Know that when the time comes to give out that you will have the strength and the means. Release unto Me the reluctance and apprehension. Know that each situation has been sent for a reason, and I shall bless. Rely on Me to bring it forth. You shall see more fruit of your labors and we shall rejoice together.

Your words, as brought forth by Me, shall bring forth the miracles you wish to see. Stick to basics. Keep your eyes on Me. My will shall prevail. Leave the melodramas to others. Keep it simple and unencumbered. Proceed with simplicity. Respond with clarity and go forth with assurance. Magnify My Word; minimize problems. Sit in the heavenlies with Me, undisturbed, unperturbed, and unafraid, resting in the peace of My love.

Light the fire of joy in your heart. Light the fire of hope springing alive through peace. Light the fire of forgiveness and love. Light shall be the burden carried of My compassion and love. It shall go forth from you as gently and easily as the breath of My Spirit. Go forth with joy, go forth with peace, go forth with love, go forth with the gifts of My Spirit. Stand tall in My love and in standing tall, shade others with My love.

Forbearance is still a virtue to be pursued and obtained. It is captured through constant and vigilant love and acceptance, unconditional love, given and received, untainted by performance orientation. No need to perform to your standards to receive your unconditional love. Give it forth liberally and unrestricted to the joy of your heart and to the joy of My heart. You shall see and experience more love than you've ever known. Reach out with acceptance and love.

Day 18

Learn to manage your emotions through forbearance and unconditional love. Acceptance in the midst of trials is truly riding the high road. The road is sparsely traveled but prepared for you. Follow it with diligence. Forsake disgust, dismay, and dissatisfaction. Follow discipline, diligence, and delight. Cover their lack and need with your love. The world waits to condemn. You accept, encourage, and love. All else slows their progress and stunts their growth in Me. Let Me rebuke. Let the world criticize, but you accept, encourage, and love.

Sing for the night is over. Sing for the new day dawns. Sing for the blessings abundant; come forth as the rising sun. The night truly is over and the brightness of the sun is shining forth its rays of healing and wholeness. I have said, the time of My visitation is upon you. Rise forth in the knowledge of My loving-kindness. A new day has dawned, a day of understanding, peace, and joy in My faithfulness. The time has come of newness and wholeness. Relish its freshness in your life. It shall not wane, but becomes increasingly fuller in scope and power. Be at peace in your heart. Doors shall open, and you shall know My direction and care. Do not worry or fret but be at peace, and let Me put the puzzle together to My Glory and to your unequaled joy. I see the way; it is strewn with roses, and you shall be pleased.

Let worry and regret be far from you, as far as the east is from the west, for unto you have I given strength and endurance to continue on the path of My choosing. I say, worry not, for I have provided for and have planned for every detail. Move forward slowly and with faith, for I am with you to sustain, comfort, and strengthen you and to guide you with tender care. It shall not be a hard path, but one filled with My love. Step out with pride in Me, and together we shall prevail. Have I not said, and has it not come to pass? I have said that you would not miss My best. So go forth with unequaled faith in the future, unafraid, free from stress and dread. Have I not said that your path is strewn with roses? And so it is. Their fragrance and beauty shall draw others to your path, and all shall rejoice.

Reach out with love and compassion. The words are not as important as the spirit. The Spirit is Mine and I shall minister. Fear not for the words, for they shall be there in power and in truth.

Mark the days as they fall one upon another, filled with blessings in abundance. None shall be lost. All shall bear My signature of love. You can rely on that. Be assured of My constant and abiding care over thee and thine. Nothing is lost. Nothing is for naught. All has worth in My eyes. See as I see with the eyes of wisdom, truth, and love. A way has been made, a way to bring forth the desires of your heart. Watch and see and rejoice in the outpouring and outflowing of My plan, direction, and blessing for and to thee and thine. The watchword is stand! Stand and rejoice!

Day 19

Strength of character comes forth through patient waiting. Patient waiting has become the vehicle through which My blessings shall come forth. Change is not easy but is necessary to bring forth growth. It comes forth slowly, developing patience and faith. Welcome change with open arms. It is a friend. When it seems that change will overwhelm you, stand back and rejoice. Be at peace, for I am with you, comforting, consoling, directing, and loving. I have fashioned the fabric of your life into a tight weave that none of My blessings might fall through. All shall come to pass at My appointed time and in My appointed way. Be at peace and rejoice, for with My perfect timing it shall all come together, nothing lacking, with perfection. Rest in that assurance.

How do you bake a cake? (*You add the ingredients one by one, mix them, bake the cake, and serve it.*) I prepare My servants the same way and then serve them to the world as a sweet aroma, drawing the world to Me. Be prepared to go forth with joy, for I have prepared you. I have baked you to perfection in the oven of My love. You shall bless and refresh, heal and restore. Yours shall be the family of God.

Balance strategy (plans) and forbearance (patience). In both are found My Spirit of truth received in peace. Both are necessary to the whole. Don't value one over the other. Step lightly with agility. It is a time of balance. Fear not. Times of refreshment shall come, and together we shall proceed.

Store up My wisdom in your heart. In due season it shall be tapped as rivers of living water, bringing health, happiness, and salvation to the hearers. In due season it shall flow. Be not impatient. Your storehouse will never run dry. It is a strengthening, nourishing, growing time.

Teach others to remain in My peace no matter what the situation. My peace is like a warm blanket on a cold night and is maintained through trust in Me. Fear and anxiety are the opposite of trust. Lay a groundwork of walking in peace, joy, and trust, which is faith. Continue to walk in My grace, and continue to hold it out for others.

Love as I Have Loved You

*This is My commandment,
that you love one another,
as I have loved you*
(John 15:12).

Day 20

Be My love! Manifest My love! Be a reflection of My love to others! Radiate My love. Be a transmitter of My love. Receive it, transmit it continuously by My Spirit. Be a life-giver. Stand in the gap for My precious ones. Let them learn by example. Peace and joy open the door to My rest brought forth by love. (God's love is straightforward, honest, gives wisdom, discernment, knowledge, peace, joy, warmth, comfort, and truth. It restores and blesses. God's love keeps life simple, not complex. It turns darkness into light. God's love puts people on solid ground, for they know they are accepted and acceptable.) Grow in My love day by day. The more you understand of My love and walk in My love, the more you can give of My love. You can only give what you have. Walk in My light that you might turn the darkness around you to light. Darkness cannot abide in the presence of light. My light and My love are one. Contained within your heart is the knowledge of My love. It is a love unhindered by time and space. It goes beyond the limited confines of the mind. It must be understood from the heart. Limited is the understanding brought forth by logic. My love is limitless. Love as I have loved you.

The ravages of time are to those who stretch with apprehension and fear. Sooth their broken spirits with My love and peace, that My understanding might bring joy. Know that I undertake even at your feeblest of efforts. Be not afraid to offer My peace in love.

Strangers see and respond to the love, peace, and joy I have painstakingly bestowed upon you and worked through you. It is My calling card. It is undeniable and irresistible. It is My light, and they are drawn by its warmth, truth, and protection. Your home shall be My lighthouse of love, an outpost drawing the lame, the deaf, and the blind to its warmth, protection, and healing love. My peace shall permeate and My joy shall sing. The walls shall ring with My joy. All who pass its threshold shall be aware of special gifts being bestowed upon them, love radiating, joy ringing, and peace permeating. They shall search you out. They shall be blessed, healed, delivered, and made whole. My ways are beyond comprehension. I have and will open doors that will make your heart sing, and together we shall shed light and healing love.

Do you remember the migrating, the moving from place to place? (*Yes, Lord, I do.*) Do you remember the mighty blessings and miracles that accompanied you in those migrations? (*I sure do, Lord.*) Do you trust Me? (*Lord, You have always proven to be trustworthy. You have never let me down.*) Then lift up your heart and rejoice, for the time of entering in has arrived. Justification by grace has become a way of life for you, depending on My grace to guide, protect, and provide. My hand of provision has opened wide for you. My timing has been perfect and My lessons have made you strong. Let your heart rejoice, for the time of entering in is at hand. Rejoice, I say, in the multitude of blessings that have been yours and the multitude of blessings that are in store.

Day 21

Settled in My Word have I made you to be by the sharing of My heart with you. The heavens open wide to the hungry, seeking heart. Continue to feed on My Word voraciously, and I shall continue to rain upon you My attributes, combined to bring you joy. Together we shall gently rain like a mist of joy upon others that they might seek and find. Rejoice in the outpouring of My Spirit upon you and yours and upon those I give you. Make their hearts sing with the good news of My love for them. The harvest shall be great. Our joy shall be great, and great shall be the outpouring of My love.

You are a fire escape. Arise and shine for the Glory of the Lord is upon you to bring forth the works of My hand and the blessings of My heart. A trumpet shall sound in Zion. Another has gone forth to comfort My people and to bring to life those at ease in Zion. Brush off your garments and stand in praise to your God who has brought you to this place of service. Magnify the Lord and give praise to the God of all creation. Let your heart sing with the knowledge and awareness of My grace and power, and all shall see My grace and My power through you. Arise and shine for the Light of the World is shining forth with life, health, and abundance of joy. My peace is with you, is in you, and shall be the foundation of My work through you.

Be a Traveler Palm, refreshing those weary travelers through life with your storehouse of refreshing, living water. Blessed shall you be as you give forth of that life-giving, living water. Lasting happiness sits at your gate this day. Invite her in. Sup with her. Know that from this day forth, My blessings shall flow over you and lead you onward in My way everlasting. Make way, for the deluge is coming of My everlasting love. Be a converter that it might be a steady flow.

My Word penetrates deeply into the inner being, bringing about results of My making. My Word molds and shapes and produces fruit that is sweet to the taste, giving life, stamina, and hope to those languishing on the sidelines. Let My Word continue to bubble forth with abundant life. Harken, harken to the sound of My voice in the still of the night, in the evening hours, in the cool of the day, in the midst of your daily activities. Tune your heart to listen, to establish an unbroken channel of communication between Me and thee. My Spirit waits for an invitation to commune.

Time stands still for those who trust. Time races with anxiety for those who don't. When time stands still nothing is lost; mistakes are not made and all is accomplished within the framework of My will. Those for whom time races with anxiety, nothing seems to go right. See that you move forward in My peace that time might stand as if still in the perfection of My will. When one's attention is strongly focused on Me, one doesn't see the unimportant disturbances to the right or to the left. The ride of trust becomes so smooth it seems as if still, but is in actuality moving quickly ahead step by step within the framework of My perfect will. Ride in trust. Ride in peace. Ride in the joy of the completion of My perfect will.

Day 22

Lighten your load. It need not be that heavy. Have I not said, "Light is the load of those who follow after Me." Set your eyes on

Me. Walk in My joy. Walk in My peace. Let Me be the arbitrator. My children walk in the assurance of My love for them. That is where their strength and resilience comes from. The assurance of that love moves them through the storms of life unscathed. Nothing can penetrate the peace and joy of My Spirit when one is fully aware of My love. No need for resentment, no need for hurt. I love you. All is well. So go forth this day with joy and peace in your heart, for I love you with a perfect and everlasting love.

I have many things to tell you, many truths for you to learn. Day by day I reach out to you and place a nugget of truth in your hand for you to ponder and mull over, turning it over and studying it as it molds your life. Take each nugget each day and let it work its weight in gold. (*Lord, sometimes it seems that I am juggling nuggets.*) I never give you more than you can handle. Thanksgiving and praise help the truths to absorb more quickly. Negative words harden the heart against the absorption of truth. Flee anything negative, the four Cs—complaining, criticizing, condemning, constricting—and emphasize the positive, cheerful, joyful, loving, and praiseworthy good report.

The light of My countenance shines on you, My child, making of you a beacon light for many to find their way to Me. Shine, shine, shine. Never let that light go out through resentment, fear, or hurt. (*I'll say, Lord, You deal with them. I haven't got the time or inclination to be upset or hurt. Lord, You heal them. I'll bless them, and carry on being a light bearer, a bearer of Your light, peace, joy, and love. I'll deal with the positives and let You deal with the negatives. Amen.*) Now you've got it, My child. Hang on to it and don't let it go. It is one of the nuggets of truth I was telling you about. I have handed it to you. You have lived it, pondered it, turned it around in your hand, and absorbed it as truth. Hang on to it and thrive and prosper.

Listen with My ears and you shall miss nothing. Listen with My ears that hear, understand, and comprehend what is being said. You will see more, understand more, and comprehend more, that I might use you more to bring healing and wholeness to My people. You must hear with My Spirit, for the natural ears hear not the cry of the heart, but only the words spoken, which are so inadequate. Hear with My ears, that you might hear what I hear, and with love and compassion give forth the answer from My heart. You shall hear, you shall understand, and you shall comprehend that together we might move with confidence to bring forth healing and wholeness to each whose heart cries out for help, even though no words are spoken and no words can cover. Respond to My nudgings and leadings with confidence and love. My attributes have been salted into your very being and now are being mined by those around you for the blessings those nuggets of pure gold will bestow. Give the nuggets freely. Make them readily available. Freely they have been given, freely give.

There are all kinds of love. Love that rejoices in the feats of others, love that sticks close through failure and pain, love that makes light of wrongs endured, love that persists against all odds for the word spoken believed. This is the love I have given you to give. Let not up when odds seem slim and defeat seems to prevail. Turn defeat into victory by claiming My truth and standing on that truth undaunted by the passing scene, for My Word stands and My promises are sure. Be not faint-hearted, but strong in your faith and belief, and strong in the love I have given you to give. Be a giver, not a taker. Give your love to others without thought of return, taking only from Me, My love, and you will never lack.

Day 23

Precious, precious, precious are My children to Me. They bring Me joy. Listen, My child, as I give to you keys for living, keys that shall see you through to the end with great glory and praise. For it shall be My Glory and My praise shining about you, drawing the multitudes to Me. Love with My love. It heals, restores, and brings forth great joy. It brings hope, gives faith, and lets them see Me. Open your heart to receive My love in greater measure. Yes, My child, be My love. Be the manifestation of My love and together we shall see others rejoice and made whole in My Name. (*How do I go about it, Lord?*) Just receive and it shall flow forth naturally to the delight of us both. Receive, receive, receive, and together we shall give freely of My love. Amongst My jewels shall you walk, never scratching nor marring them, but gently polishing them to brilliancy with love.

See Me, not in the corporate, but in the individual. Be mindful of My love to you. (*You love me the way I want to be loved.*) Love others in the same way. Don't point out wrongs and slights. Pray. Be a praise-giver, not a slight-harborer. Be a restorer. Be a waterer and a bearer of blessings. Be My love and My light to the brethren. Be assured of My love and you will not lack for their love.

You know the ways of My Spirit. You have tasted of its richness and its Glory. Heed well the words of My Spirit that they be ingrained into your life, compromising not their power. Painstakingly I have sealed My words to your heart, making of your heart a storehouse of My words and of My power to change lives. Languish not beneath the pressures of this life, but draw on My words and let them explode in your heart, bringing strength, soundness, and exuberance, for they are life-giving Words, always available to spur you on to bring forth My will. Languish not, for it brings weakness and death instead of life and health. Be strong in My Spirit. Bring forth songs of Zion. Bring them forth in joy and in the framework of My love, strength, joy, and fullness of life. Be a life-giver. Walk in My strength. Walk in the abundance of My love, and let your heart sing with the strength of that love.

Radiate My Peace

You will keep him in perfect peace,
whose mind is stayed on You,
because he trusts in You
(Isaiah 26:3).

Day 24

Radiate My Peace! All seek My peace. All search for its richness and fulfillment. Make it readily available and easily read in your countenance and in your life. My peace is the bait held forth in joy and with promise. Liberally give it forth in My Name. All that come in contact with it shall be affected by it, warmed and softened that My love might be received. Light the fires of understanding in many through your constant, persistent peace. Give it forth to the Glory of My Name.

Never despair! Never give up! For I see the end from the beginning, bathed in the light of My love. Victory shines forth brilliantly in My eyes. Share the knowledge of that victory in Me, for it is yours to share in all its fullness of joy. The choice is always yours. Rejoice and be glad, for I have told you the outcome is victory, or languish and be sad for lack of commitment to My Word. Commitment to My Word always brings victory. Walk in the light of My love. It brings joy. Go forth singing, laughing, praising, rejoicing, and standing on My Word of victory.

A picture is worth a thousand words. I have made of your life a picture of My love, made manifest upon the screen (fabric) of your life. Keep that love in sharp focus that the screen of your life might project unceasingly the reality of My love to you, through you, and for My people. I have said in the past, "Rejoice in the becoming." Now I say, "Rejoice in the projecting of My love. Be the reflection of My love to others."

Minister My peace and love to others as I have ministered My love and peace to you. See them through My eyes. Let Me love them through you, judging not, but accepting them on their ground. Accepting them totally and letting Me take care of the unnecessary props. I bring forth righteousness in each one. That is not your part. Your part is to accept and love them where they are. My peace I give to you that you might love without condemnation, frustration, or confusion.

The ways of My Spirit are apparent to all who listen and watch. Let your life sing within the perfection and beauty of the framework of the symphony I have created you to be. Enjoy the beauty, the perfect timing, and the music of your life, and others shall enjoy it also and be blessed. Be the symphony I have created you to be through trust, contentment, love, peace, and joy in Me, and faith that I have written the score to perfection. Blessed is the one who allows Me to create of their life a symphony.

Day 25

Stand firm your ground, the ground gained through struggle and determined resolve. Let not up your stance of faith and let Me continue to lead you on to higher ground of accomplishment. Hang on to victories won by repenting of sin and laying the groundwork for even higher achievements in My Name. (*How do I lay the groundwork, Lord?*) Stay in My Word. Listen astutely to My guiding voice and let your heart sing in the joy of your salvation. Stamina comes through commitment to My Word. A legacy of strength is yours through My Word. Strength, stability, stamina, and reliability all come through My Word. Drink deeply and voraciously. Drink deeply of the Well of Life.

The minds of men cause problems that don't exist. Put your mind at rest knowing that I am with you to discern and to know My direction and leading. Let go of the distraction, heaviness, and confusion of mind and soul. Let Me sooth the frayed resolve. "Mind over matter," it has been said, but I say, "Spirit over mind." Let My Spirit reign, and peace shall descend and conquer all confusion. Resist the temptation to let your mind dwell on the unimportant. Let it soar in realms of Glory.

Listen and hear My words of wisdom to you. Go forth in the might of My power through you. It is there to strengthen, motivate, lead and guide, sustain and propel you to your destiny as planned by Me. Let go of past ruts and inadequate ways of thinking and reacting. Let Me bring forth a new way of thinking, moving, and reacting, for there are new and expanded experiences on the horizon demanding new ways of response. Lay before Me the old, outgrown responses and motivations. Now go forth unmoved by negative impute, but moved only by positive love given forth by My Spirit.

Strong and stable have been My ways for you, brought forth through struggle and faith. Continue on My child, for I have brought life and light to your very being and together we shall bring light and life to others who struggle without faith. The prisoners shall be set free to soar by My Spirit. Get ready to fly. Get ready to soar and explore and to have the ride of your life. I have brought you thus far for the purpose of the expression of My Spirit of love. Together we shall enfold My precious ones in the warmth, peace, joy, and freedom of My love.

I shall continue to lead you in the blessing of and intercession for My people, and together we shall see miracles and joy abounding. Within the framework of My love I gently mold, shape, and mature you, and them, into fine polished gems of My making, fit to shine forth with radiance and beauty the attributes of My Spirit. Rejoice, My child, for each day brings forth added radiance and polish to My finished work, and none shall stay My hand, but I shall be glorified in My creation. Enjoy each day as it comes, confident in My ability to lead and guide you with nothing missing or lacking. Go forth each day with assurance in My loving care over your life.

Rejoice in the here and now. Take from each day the nectar provided. Take the nectar from each day, digest it and let it become honey for others. Take from this day a full measure of My love, peace, joy, wisdom, discernment, and My Word, and it shall be given out as the honey of My Word, discernment, wisdom, joy, peace and My love. Give it forth liberally. The more nectar you take in each day, the more you have to give out. Let it flow like a river of life to you and to others.

Day 26

Racing, racing, racing, racing, straining to reach the finish line. Straining, racing against time to accomplish all the mind finds to do.

Have I not said, "Simply be the manifestation of My peace. Be the manifestation of My love. Let Me be the projector that moves you along in the direction of victory." Strain not! Race not! Simply be My peaceful, loving, joyful manifestation of My Spirit. My Spirit strives not. It races not. It is! Let Me show you how to be by letting down the mask of peace, love, and joy and taking up a life of praise and worship, which brings forth the constantly producing fruits of love, peace, and joy abounding. My peace, love and joy, brought forth through praise and worship, does not drain and cause weariness. It refreshes and brings forth constant fruit in your life and the lives of others.

Sit straight, stand straight, think straight, and speak straight from the heart. Be straightforward, My child, and My Sprit shall be magnified through you. Don't worry, fret not, but instead let Me make the adjustments. You be faithful to speak and I will be faithful to act. Labor not to be a light. Simply shine by the power of My Holy Spirit. My light shall go forth and accomplish all that I have ordained for it to accomplish. Rejoice, My child. Rejoice and go forth this day in the light of My Spirit and truth.

My heart sings for you, My child. I have planted, protected, and lovingly provided for your growth and care. You have developed and grown, and together we have rejoiced as each victory was won. I have stabilized you and brought forth from your being gifts and attributes of My Spirit. I am well-pleased with My creation. There is more to be added, more to be subtracted, but together we shall rejoice as each day brings forth new growth and new victories.

I have surrounded you with prayer and love. When one strikes out who feels neither, respond with compassion, for My truth will win out and My compassion shall rule and bind up hurts and fears. Reach out unafraid of repercussions. Reach out and love and let Me take care of the results. Proceed with caution, but proceed with love and acceptance for the one who feels none. I am with you, My child, to bring healing and wholeness. Let Me lead, and together we shall see miracles abounding, love and joy surrounding your life at every turn.

My child, listen to My footsteps as I walk beside you or in front of you. If beside, we walk, talk, and fellowship. If ahead, follow closely, for we forge new paths and you must follow closely. Hear My footsteps ahead of you now. Listen closely, follow closely. Be alert and listening for My every move. It isn't hard. Listen, watch Me up ahead and follow. Speak My words, sleep My words, follow My words and be My words. The time is now to be what I have called you to be, My lifeline of hope, peace, and love, creatively walking by My Spirit of praise and worship. I have called you to be a lighthouse of rest by My Spirit of praise which brings peace. Life and light spring forth from My Spirit of peace. Be a peace-giver and together we shall see lives changed, mountains moved, and My Kingdom proclaimed.

When you feel the blow of defeat, I always turn it to victory. Time after time, I have been to you the Rock of Gibraltar, being that strong bulwark of peace and stability. I am your stronghold and I will not forsake you. Take on a new identity in Me, Jehovah-jireh—Jehovah will provide.

Day 27

Stay away from greed. It robs the heart of stability and peace. It places a noose around the heart, taking it captive. Wrestle not with greed. Let it be. Don't make peace with it. Stay away. You can forgive a snake for being a snake, but it is still a snake and if you come close, you will get bitten. Let moderation be your motto, never excess. Greed is brought about by fear, fear that I will not provide your needs. Lay aside your fears and walk at peace with Me and with others. My peace is My gift to you brought about by your trust in Me.

Show forth My light in greater ways. Hide it not under a bushel. I have revealed to you many truths, truths that bring freedom and light. Shine forth that light which is truth and freedom, and it shall make your pathway even brighter. I have blessed you with many blessings designed to lead you ever closer to My heart and love. Straight and narrow is the path, but wide is My love. Walk in the wideness of My love and you will follow the straight, narrow path.

Many times I have protected you from the realities of life. Now your ears shall hear, your eyes shall see, and you shall respond as I would have you respond in wisdom and in truth. Fear not the realities of life. They cannot harm you. They only teach greater truths of My Kingdom and bring you into greater heights in My Spirit. I shall lead and guide you gently. Be not afraid, but let Me show you greater realms of service by My Spirit, and together we shall set the captives free. Continue on in faith. Let Me be your support as you encounter uncomfortable situations, for together we shall see mountains move and far greater strides shall be made than ever before in your growth and maturity. Blessed assurance is the key. Go forth confident in My ability to bring you through to victory and fulfillment.

Stay close to My heart, My child, for there is safety and peace. Bring to Me your fears and frustrations and let Me put out the fire that rages within, for to Me it is a simple thing, whereas to you, it seems to rage on without recourse. Let Me provide you with answers that bring peace and calm. Let Me manifest My wisdom in each situation that the waters of life might be calm and the situations victorious. My little child, come quickly to My lap for counsel and comfort. Let Me soothe the fevered brow and lighten the load, and at the end of each day I will say, "Well done thou trusted and faithful servant." My peace is yours, My child. Take it to your heart and rejoice in My faithfulness and loving-kindness.

Now let the light of My countenance shine upon you from this day forward, undiminished by disappointment or discouragement. For in the light of My countenance there can be no discouragement or disappointment, only the joy of My Presence and promise, and the song of My Spirit of love. Let it sing strongly in your life unabated. Be neither grieved nor remorseful, but walk before Me with a pure heart, with hope and trust in My sustaining love. Stand before Me confident that I will uphold you, sustain you, and bring you through to victory.

Rest in the Glory
of My Presence

*Now to Him who is able to keep you
from stumbling, and to present you faultless
before the presence of His glory with exceeding joy*
(Jude 24).

Day 28

Rest, rest, My child, in the Glory of My Presence. Weighed down by doubt and unbelief, one cannot soar, but loosed through song, one can soar in the heavenlies with Me. Soar, My child, soar and let Me soothe frayed wings that have been battered by the winds that have blown un-abated. Be at peace, My child. Rest in My love.

People, places, and things are the building blocks of a life. Love, faith, and honor are the building blocks of the Spirit. All are given by My hand. All are received by choice by you. Trust Me to give them all to you and trust Me to help you to receive.

Fill your life with song. Come into My Presence with singing. Glo-rious and magnificent song brings joy and life to My children who lan-guish in the heat of the battle. Restrain not the song of praise in your heart. Let it sing with glorious abandon. Let My peace reign in your heart, as I replace frustration and confusion with joy and light, as you sing your praises to Me. Go forth now unencumbered by doubt, guilt, and confusion. Go forth in trust and faith that what I have begun in you I will complete. I will not abandon you. You are safe within My loving hand, and what you see as failure, I see as growth. Go forth, My child, with abandon, in the safety of My love. Languish not, for I see, restore, and hasten to lift you up when you lose your footing. Get right back up in confidence.

Amongst My flowers grow thorns, but they cannot affect the beauty and blessing of those flowers. For My sun, rain, and soil cause them to flourish, grow, and shine forth My Glory. Trust Me to continue to nourish, love, and protect you and cause you to grow and flourish. Be not con-cerned about the thorns among the flowers. Let Me deal with them. You keep your face raised to the Sonshine of My smile and soak up the rays of the Son. Let the rain of My Spirit refresh you and the soil of My love en-fold you and cause you to flourish and grow. Be at peace in the Sonshine of My love. Sing in the Sonshine.

Stand guard on the portals of your heart that they not betray you, that evil not be allowed to enter through frustration, fear, or injustice. Keep a clean heart, no matter what is going on around you. Be aware and alert to the spirits of pride and self-pity that will try to creep in the back door from feelings of hurt and injustice. Let it not be said that you became an accuser. Let it be said that you held steady and firm to the end, extending your hand of friendship and love. Straightforward and full of truth and discernment you shall be, but it shall be with no hint of condemnation or struggle. It shall be in My strength, brought forth with love, My truth and My Word, to bring forth healing and restoration. So shall it be. Go forth in faith, for I go before you, preparing the ground to bring forth healing and peace.

Day 29

Don't seek for an answer and clear it with Me. Seek the answer from Me and it shall be clear!

Remain at peace, My child, for I have not stopped working in your life and shall continue to bring forth miracles and solutions to problems that seem to loom and will extract peace and joy. Remain in My peace and joy, for I am the problem solver; I have placed you where I want you, to confirm and bring forth My will. Praise continues to be your safeguard, and peace continues to be the barometer of your walk with Me. Continue on in strength, fortitude, and determination to see My will brought forth and My ways fulfilled. Worry not for the future. Simply trust Me for today. Rejoice in the present and My care for you, and those you love. The pathway is flooded with light, and you shall not stumble or fall. My Spirit of love shall continue to uphold, sustain, train, and guide. I love you, My child! Amen!

Intimidation and insecurity are indications of a heart removed from the absolute knowledge of My love and acceptance. Let it not be said, My child, that you did not know of and accept all of My love, acceptance, and confidence in you. Let it be said that you walk in grace and truth brought forth by a total acceptance of My love and acceptance of her. You walk in grace and beauty, this one who knows the Father's heart of love, for you have inherited all of the Father's treasure, secured for you from the foundation of the earth. You can walk around it, beside it, or past it, or you can walk in full acceptance, trust in, and full receivership of My love, blessings, acceptance, and inheritance.

See the birds, how they fly with such freedom? (*Yes, Lord.*) The vastness of My universe is theirs to enjoy. They sing victoriously with great joy and trust in their freedom. There is strength in freedom. Singing brings joy to the hearer. Freedom with wisdom brings life. Restraints with fear bring death. Measure your life by My Spirit of freedom within your heart. Freedom to love, freedom to rejoice, freedom to receive My words of life, freedom to give My words of life, freedom to walk in faith and trust, freedom to thank Me in all things, and freedom to *be* all that I have created you to be. Let Me continue to help you walk in the Glory of My freedom. Let the freedom of My Spirit ring in your heart with great abounding joy. There is much ahead, My child, and it depends on My Spirit of freedom residing with power within your heart.

A tree grows strong by nourishment (My Word, written and spoken), faith (trust in My Word of truth), and sunlight (My love), the natural outgrowth being joy and thanksgiving. Be that beautiful healthy tree of My choosing, brought forth to bless and comfort My people, and I shall make of you a tree of strength and beauty that cannot be toppled or harmed. Be My tree of righteousness, the planting of the Lord. I have planted you, watered you, nourished, and sustained you. Grow, thrive, and rejoice evermore!

Lay down your abilities before Me and let Me develop them to their fullest. Let Me promote and let lay dormant along the way, for I shall prosper and bring forth your talents at the appropriate time. There shall be no limits put upon My assigned blessings and the use of those talents. Fear not for their use. Let Me use them for My Glory, and I shall bring forth an abundant harvest from each talent at the appointed time and place.

Day 30

Remain under the constant care and abiding love of My outspread wings of protection and direction. Fear not, My little one. Let Me lead and bring forth an abundant harvest in your life with nothing lacking. Silence in your heart the doubts and the fears, for they are not of or from Me. Set your heart and your thoughts on Me and let Me be your perfect guide. What I have started in you I will finish. I will not abandon you. Hold fast your ground. Waver not. I have put within you a singing heart, which shall be revealed in My time.

My child, stake your claim by My Spirit and stick to it like glue. Seek Me daily for My Word and promises and let them be your pillar of strength. My strength is your strength and My Word is that strength. Stand on it, My child, unwavering, and strength shall be yours. To take away My Word is to take away your strength. Let it saturate your being. Let it be the meat that energizes and moves you. My Word—your life and being! Rejoice in the Word that is in your heart. It is there to stay and causes you to grow in strength each day. Go forth in the strength of My Word.

My right hand of blessing is upon you, My child. Let it rest comfortably in faith and trust. Let it strengthen your inner being with much joy and continued peace. Let your mind be a place of peace, unperturbed by agitated voices that clamor it won't get done—for it will all be accomplished with ease. My peace I give to you in abundant measure. Let it rest on you in fullness. Resist the temptation to be agitated. Let My will come forth in the fullness of time. Resist the frustration that tries to take hold. Rest in My peace of heart and let My hand of love guide and direct your pathway with nothing missing. Praise continues to be your safeguard and peace continues to be the barometer of your walk with Me.

Stand straight and tall and be a sturdy ambassador of My Kingdom, undaunted by blight, persecution, unloveliness, or criticism, for I guide your ship. I set the wheels in motion that propel you along and I set the boundaries beyond which you will not go. You answer to Me and Me only, and I have set your course for victory and blessing for you and for those whose lives you touch. Fear not their reactions, their neglect, their failures, or their critical spirits. Be gracious and loving. Give them space, for I am molding them and am responsible for their growth too. Be flexible and resilient in My hands and watch Me bring forth a beautiful life—yours. Continue to be a beacon light of love, compassion, and gentleness, with a forgiving, spacious spirit.

Look out at the panorama before you. Soak in its beauty. See the ups and the downs, the hills, mountains, and valleys, and the areas clouded by haze, but it is all beautiful. So is your life. Every day, every hour, every minute, every second is a beautiful product of My perfect plan for your life. Some meanings are hidden by the soft haze, but they too are important and beautiful in My sight. The ups and downs, the hills, mountains, and valleys form the beauty that is so pleasing to the eye. So it is with you. I am forming beauty in your life, beauty that will last forever and will be a blessing forever. Relish and enjoy the formation. I am imprinting My beauty upon your body, soul, and spirit. Enjoy the process through faith, love, peace, joy, and trust. My very best is yours to enjoy. Continue on, My child, with My grace sustaining and leading you. My peace leads you forth to victory.

Day 31

Struggle not, My child, to understand the coming events. Let Me filter them through My love and make of them a masterpiece in your life. Struggle not to maintain control over the events of your life. Walk in My peace. I will bring order and understanding and eliminate the unnecessary. You can depend on that. Now go forward with a light heart, depending on My love to bring you through to victory. Let not distractions detain you along the way by bringing depression and disillusionment before you. Resist and destroy their power by My Word of love and the sacrifice of praise. I love you, My child. Let that truth resound in your heart and prevail.

A steady commitment brings results and victory. Maintain a steady gait. Continue on with faith in My ability to bring forth and bless. Fear not, but trust My steady guiding arm to sustain and guide you. Struggle is counterproductive. Press on with a steady gait, with confidence and the knowledge that I am in control and all is well. Stand tall in My Spirit and rejoice in the present for it will bring forth the future with nothing missing. Let My peace permeate your body, soul, and spirit. Let this time of quietness work its peace within your whole being. Receive all that I give and rejoice.

I am working within your heart a new sense of peace and completeness. Time is a continuous outworking of My will within your life. Enjoy the trip along the way. Don't bolt but be at peace and enjoy the view. Let Me permeate your being with peace and beauty. Let go of frenzied activity. Peace, peace, marvelous peace, coming down from the Father above. Enfold it to your heart as a friend. Time enough for much activity. This is a time of peace. Relish it, My child.

Arise, let your light shine. Hide it not under a bushel to retreat in darkness. Let it shine brilliantly that all may see and rejoice in its brilliant and warming light, for the Glory of the Lord has risen upon you. Let it shine forth unhindered by circumstances beyond your control. Let My Spirit of light control you, not circumstances sent to trip you up. Refuse their power by continuing to walk in My power. You will find ways to bless, to bring forth the best in others with graciousness. The heavens proclaim the Glory of God, and the Glory of God shall be proclaimed through you as you let the ministry of peace, love, and contentment have its way in you.

I Am the God
Who Healeth Thee

Bless the Lord, O my soul;
and all that is within me,
bless His holy name!
Bless the Lord, O my soul,
and forget not all His benefits:
Who forgives all your iniquities,
Who heals all your diseases

(Psalm 103:1-3).

Day 32

Have you not seen and heard many things this day and in days past? Lay them all aside and let Me speak words of truth to your heart and mind. Shallow words bring frustration and fear. Words spoken by My Spirit bring peace, serenity, and confidence in the midst of trial. Let Me speak words of truth to your heart to bring confidence and right thinking. The days ahead herald a width and abundance of knowledge and fellowship with Me. Lengthen and strengthen your fellowship with Me. Let it be a fluid, continuous outgrowth of your love for Me. Let it touch each experience of your life with joy. Let it be the motivating force behind each action and reaction. Let it shine forth from your life with ever-increasing power, for I have proclaimed and shall bring to pass in your life more miracles than you have dreamed of and shall establish them with love. Fear not, My little one, for I have you in the palm of My hand. Rest and wrestle not. Be at peace. I am the God who healeth you.

Worry not! Weary not! Go forth in confidence! Carry not the burden of fear, for I go with you to pave the way. Struggle not with apprehensions, for I shall heal thee My way. The scalpel shall bring healing. I shall not abandon you, but shall bring you forth healthy and whole in My Presence. Release unto Me your fears of abandonment. I shall be with you, protecting you. Let Me heal you in this way. I shall be glorified in your midst. Proclaim My goodness!

I have lengthened and strengthened your tent stakes in preparation of many events and responsibilities still to come your way. Strength shall be your by-word, a way of life for you, brought forth by My hand of provision and blessing. Continue to store up My Word in your heart, for it shall shore up areas of weakness and bring forth a seasoned warrior in My army worthy of your calling. Stay strong in your convictions, for I shall not let you down. Total healing shall be yours to enjoy and blossom forth in. My promise is sure and secure, and together we shall proceed in faith and wholehearted love for one another and for others I have given you to love. Continue on, My child, in full abandonment to My Spirit within you. I love you, My child.

Hold your head up high and value My Word to you above all words that come to confuse. I will be magnified in your life. I will fulfill the commitments I have made to you and you shall see the fulfillment and full completion of My Word to you. Languish not under the burden of unresolved confusion. Let My Word to you be yea and verily, for I have committed to restore and make whole and to facilitate future ministry in My Name. Fear not, for I am with you. I comfort and uphold you and lead you beside still waters. Rest and drink deeply from the fresh flow, and together we shall see new vistas of service. Make of your heart a resting place for My Word that it might go forth with power and simplicity.

Day 33

Amongst My jewels you are, and as each crisis is met, new sparkle and radiance is added to bring forth My beauty. You shall see My hand of love opening doors that seem closed and making known blessings that seem hidden.

A stiff breeze has blown through, blowing things about, leaving confusion and distrust. Lay down your right to your own feelings of rejection and focus on their need for confirmation and respect. Grace and love shall prevail and bring about much needed understanding and peace. Watch for it, for My hand of love and power is extended. Release it to Me and watch Me work.

Step over the rocks, the obstacles put in your path, and be at peace. Many are the obstacles to fall on, but I say to you, be at peace and rejoice in My steadfast deliverance. The wages of war is victory in My service, for you walk in service to the King of kings and Lord of lords and nothing shall come near you that cannot be turned to victory. I have sent forth My Word to you and it is, "The Word of the Lord brings victory, not defeat!" You shall walk victoriously in My light and abundance. Stand and see the salvation of the Lord, your

God. Walk in faith, knowing that I am with you and the plots laid by the enemy shall fail and come to naught.

Rejoice, for I am bringing to you My abundance of unequaled freedom to love as I love, to sing with abandon by My Spirit of praise, thanksgiving, and healing, My healing to the hearers. Freedom it shall be, for you are My dispenser of freedom, My ambassador of freedom. But first, you shall be free, free to give without fear of not receiving, for you shall receive from Me! Be free, My child, be free from anxiety and fear. Be free to trust Me for your care.

Tell them, tell them for Me that I love them! Loose them from their boxed-in feelings of worthlessness and impotence. Let them know that with My love they are powerhouses. Change their fears to can do's. I have heard their cries in the night and I am releasing them to be My ambassadors of love, unhampered by tradition and negative words. Show them, My child, by your words of victory, brought forth by My love, the realms of victory in store for them as they walk victoriously into and through the freedom of My love. I am with you to direct your words and thoughts, and together we shall see the bound set free.

Enlargement and encouragement, two words that complement each other in their power and scope. As you encourage others, there is an enlargement of their vision to see beyond their pain and discouragement, beyond their limited vision of truth. I have broadened your scope of truth and brought you from limited vision to a place of enlarged vision to see the pain in others beyond their pleasant exterior. Many shall I bring to you who have the need for love and encouragement to penetrate their outer shell. Watch for them as I bring them your way. Set My people free from the bondages that beset them and keep them from a victorious walk with Me.

Day 34

Reflect back and see Me in every circumstance of your life. See, I am doing a new thing in your life to bring forth much fruit and an abundance of love. I have brought you thus far, and as you stretch out your wings to fly once more, I reach out to you with peace, serenity, and faith to complete the transition. Blessed is he who cometh in the name of the Lord. You are My bouncing ball. It bounces with joy and abandon wherever I take it, inflated by My Spirit of love, without a care, no holding back. My bouncing ball brings life wherever it goes and brings with it the gifts of My Spirit. Now go forth unafraid, knowing I, your Father, care for you.

Charge My people to know Me with intimacy and love. Hesitate not to bring forth experiences that praise and glorify My Name. Lay down your right to yourself. Lay that right at My feet and I will bless you and bring you peace, peace brought forth by relinquishment. Music sings in the life that is relinquished. It sings with abandon. Tremendous things lie ahead. Relinquishment shall bring them forth.

I have enlisted you in My army, fully prepared to follow instructions and to move victoriously in My sight. Little have you known of the strategic plans backing you up. Little have you seen of the preparations and minute details prepared and executed on your behalf. But now as you go forth prepared and preserved by My hand of love, you shall execute and establish My Word and My work by My Spirit of love. Go forth unafraid, fully prepared to *see, be,* and *do.* Three diverse actions brought forth by love.

I have raised you up to be strong, resilient, and quietly assured of My care over you. I shall say you, "stand," and you shall stand, "move" and you shall move, "rebuke" and you shall rebuke. I shall strengthen your resolve and straighten your backbone. I shall create you to be a mighty warrior in My army of love. (*What about the frustration and resentment, Lord?*) Strings from the past may try to tie you down and incapacitate, but I say to you, "Tie them into beautiful bows of acceptance and they cannot trip you up." Cares and worries fade away as one rests in My love.

Set your eyes on Me and follow My every move by listening closely and maintaining a watchful eye. Clear and safe is the road ahead, and peace shall abound as you rest in My love. Gratitude oils the wheels that propel you forward and gives you wings to fly. Soar, My child, with eagle's wings and rejoice in My loving-kindness. Strain not to see ahead, for I see ahead and it is good. Relax and struggle not. See, I have sustained you thus far. I shall continue to fashion and create beauty in your life and give it purpose and joy. Trust Me to continue to bless you, lead and guide you, and to open and close doors of My choosing. You are blessed, My child. Be at home in My arms of love.

Fill your life with My music, joy, and song, and splash it onto others with freedom and liberality. A life filled with joy and song has no room for criticism and negativism. Laughter pushes out darkness.

Day 35

Lightning strikes where it may, and many of My servants shall receive lightning bolts of My Spirit to bring them forth in these last days. Know that you will not be left behind. The past, present, and future blend together to bring forth My perfect will and the beauty of My creative power in your life. You have stood at the door and knocked, and I say to you, "Enter in and taste of the banquet set for you that you might go out singing, rejoicing, and giving forth of the abundance of My love." Peace leads the way, love makes a way, and joy secures the way!

Know that I will always be there to meet you as you step forth, faithful in My service. The Words of My Spirit will truly pour forth from you in abundance, and the well will never run dry, but will always run clear, fresh, and unpolluted, kept clear and pure by love. Judge not that you be not judged, but give forth a pure stream of My love.

Tumultuous times lie ahead, but My servants ride the crest of the wave and are not crushed. It is an exhilarating ride and witnessed by many as you are visible to all. Ride that wave with your hair flying victoriously and with a song of praise and thanksgiving ringing from your heart and lips.

Forbearance is still a virtue and to be pursued. But with forbearance must be love and wisdom. Love will steady forbearance, and wisdom will guide it. Stand steady and firm, and let not up your steady stance of strength, strength upon the strong foundation of My Word. Whisk confusion out the window. Steady strength and assurance are your portion. I will deal with inconsistencies. You be consistent in Me. I calm the storm and still the angry seas and bring justification and vindication. Fear not, but continue on day by day. I am with you!

Words spoken in due season illuminate dark corners and secure broken and war-scarred walls, bringing peace where there was no peace and security where all seemed lost. Listen, discern, digest, and proclaim My Word and My Light to My Glory. Healing and shoring up shall begin and you shall see My little ones step from the darkness into the light. Light and darkness are as one when My Word comes upon the scene, for I make the darkness light.

Day 36

True identity comes from Me. Seek your identity from Me and My Word. Security and solidification come from time spent with Me. Seek to further know Me that you might know yourself. See how precious well-being has been stolen. Return to being quiet in My Presence. Striving and struggling fall away, and the water is peaceful again.

Facts and figures bombard the mind, but truth comes from the Spirit. Seek to know My truth. Change amplifies truth and brings it to the foreground. Truth is stifled by tradition and stagnation. See, I have brought you through much change. It has challenged you and stretched you and caused you to grow. Change is the door through which truth enters and is recognized. Change has expanded your world, and brought light and illumination to that world. Your world will continue to change, expand, broaden, and be illumined by My truth and love.

Fear not for the future. It is held securely by My hand of love. I have led you thus far with perfection and care. Would I allow you now to stray beyond My perfect will for you? No, a thousand times, no! Say to your heart, "My God is powerful and capable of changing my heart and plans and setting my face like a flint in the right direction." Powerful is the word to describe My pathway for you, highlighted along the way with joy, laughter, and delight. Say to your heart, "I will not doubt the power of My Lord to establish my way and bring me along the path of His choosing." The pathway is clearly marked by Me, and I will not allow the enemy to rob you of any of its delights. Trust Me to secure your way and bring you safely to its completion.

Be Set Free to Bless and Comfort My People

"Comfort, yes, comfort My people!"
says your God
(Isaiah 40:1).

Day 37

I have made you stable and secure. Faint not within your spirit from the strain, but mount up as on eagle's wings, and begin to soar again in the heavenlies, unfettered by the strains and restraints of earth. Begin to fly again, My child, and worry not over the details of this life. Leave the details in My hands. They are inconsequential to you. I have them well in hand. I will handle them. You simply fly with freedom, grace, and trust in My ability to see you through each appointed junction and upheaval in the road. Worry not, I say again, but begin to fly again with peace, joy, and abandonment to My love and protection over you. Be at peace and remember, I am your Creator, the perfecter and director of all things pertaining to you. I have said in the past that you will not miss My best for you. By My power, it is yours to enjoy.

Fear of pain constricts and restricts one's growth in Me. Praise, worship, and thanksgiving gives one heavenly blinders, loosing one to walk in joy, peace, and total confidence in My ability to protect and lead. Fear paralyzes. Faithful praise amplifies My love and protection. Leadership must walk shielded by My protection of love, brought forth by the shield of praise. Neglect and regret. Incline and shine.

Blessed, blessed, I say, are My people entrusted with My Word. They are like a well-watered spring bringing forth bubbling, life-giving enthusiasm and life from My heart. They shrink not back during trials but forge ahead and make headway, even when others say, "Too bad." Go forth now with confidence and ever-growing faith in My ability to see you through to victory in every circumstance and to confirm and make known My propensity to My people. Together we shall continue to rejoice and see fruit spring forth in every season of life.

In a multitude of ways I have shown you My love. In a multitude of ways show your love to others. Redeem the time through constant intercession and praise. Join in with the angels in song brought forth through a heart filled with thanksgiving and praise.

Trials and testing magnify My faithfulness and love and enlarge the heart to give. Comfort My people! Lasting happiness is yours as you bless and comfort My people. See, I have led and comforted you that you might become a wide resting place for others. Trials and tribulation strengthen the character, giving the strength and tenderness necessary to comfort My people. Know that I will bless and comfort you.

Day 38

Sing forth and proclaim the Word of the Lord. Let it ring in your heart, and it shall be proclaimed from your life. There will be no doubt as to who is your Lord and to whom you owe your allegiance, for the truth of your heart and life shall shine forth from your countenance and shall set the captives free. Fear not for the future, for it is in My hands, secure from false reasonings and misunderstandings. My truth reigns in your life and My love reigns secure over it. So be at peace and let the burdens roll off like the dead weights that they are. Choose to be free of them. Choose to rejoice in the now and be released from unnecessary battles of the mind. Be set free in Jesus' Name!

Stretched, stretched you have been. Stretched to bring forth life by My Spirit. You have allowed the stretching to take place that you might be aware of and understand the workings of My Spirit. You have learned straightforwardness, patience, peace in the midst of the storm, forgiveness, faithfulness, perseverance, and diplomacy that you might come forth strong. Straightforward determination has served you well. You will find that you are prepared to do My bidding. In the past I have asked for dogged determination. In the present you have found that My word to you has been sacrifice. Now you will find the fruit of your labors and it will taste sweet. Be assured that the rewards far outweigh the sacrifice.

Stand fast, My child, unwavering, solid on the foundation of truth I have built for you, complete to withstand any and all storms. My faithfulness has and shall continue to sustain you through thick and thin, and the blessings of My heart shall continue to delight you and cause you joy. Fortitude has become a way of life for you, sustained by an inner peace, brought forth by joy. I am making you into a streamliner who can move swiftly and smoothly through life unhampered by the tricks of the enemy. Love, peace, joy, and wisdom propel the streamliner and keep it moving swiftly and smoothly, constantly moving by My Spirit of truth and freedom, bearing Good News.

Trace your footsteps and see that there is a pattern, a direction, and a plan. Beautiful are the feet of those who bring Good News to the captives. Stand fast, My child, for I have not forsaken you, but are raising you to new heights for My Glory. Rejoice and be glad and repeat after Me, "My God is an awesome God. Nothing is too hard for Him. He brings light in the darkness and prepares a way through the wilderness. Magnificent and beyond comprehension are His ways."

(*Lord, where do we go from here?*) Straightforward, unhindered by the past. Complete the job set before you with honor and praise. My light will shine before you, leading, guiding, and illuminating the dark corners and bringing them to light. Rejoice, for the times of testing have ceased their power over you, and a new day shines brightly before you. Carry not the hindrances of the past into the present and future. Leave them in the past and move on to better, more fruitful days. Sail on, My child! Sail on!

Stretch forth your hand to receive from Me faith to fulfill all that I have commissioned you to do and all that I have secured for you to possess. The stakes are large and the fulfillment great. The battle has been long and hard, but the message goes forth unabated to My people with love. Stand fast, My people, and see the fulfillment of My plan come to pass, to My Glory and for your blessing.

Day 39

Singleness of mind, purpose, and devotion have brought you thus far. Say to your heart, "Heart, be steadfast and immovable, proclaiming the words and intent of the Lord's heart to His people, for the blessings of His heart shall fall upon them immeasurably and without repentance. Pray to the Lord of the harvest to send forth His workers, to send forth an abundance of workers, to bring forth the fulfillment of His Word." For He hath said, "I will cause you to grow, prosper, and be a light, and those languishing in the darkness shall come to the light and find warmth, healing, and salvation for their souls." Rejoice, for the day has come, and many shall see, rejoice, and find release from the darkness and come into My marvelous light. See, I have made a way through the wilderness. Rejoice and sing My praises to a hungry people.

Strain not at gnats. The Spirit of the Lord ministers peace in the quietness, in the center of My perfect will. Release all unrelinquished frustration and hurts and let Me rewrite the script to include much needed peace and prosperity. Relinquish all sense of panic and uneasiness. Release unto Me all worries, cares, and negative responses, and let Me carry the ball to the winning of the game. Be refreshed and reclaim your peace and faith in My ability to bring forth success in My Name.

Speak forth the words that I shall give you to speak. They shall be words bathed with forgiveness. Worry not, but leave it to Me to bring forth with clarity and truth. Remain firm and resolute and abstain from scathing remarks. Let Me lead with love and forgiveness. Let the record show that you came with gentleness and a right spirit.

Be settled to know God reigns and the cares of this world will not cause you grief but will buoy you up and cause you to see Jesus and to know His gentle hand of encouragement and love. Hope has sprung alive, once again, in your heart, a flame that shall burn unabated. Strong words deter and bring to light injustices. Rest assured that words spoken to bring light to the darkened places have found their mark. My peace I give unto you and My sense of right shall prevail. Go forth unafraid and unashamed, for My Spirit goes before you lighting a way through the darkness and creating beauty from ashes.

Seasons change and with the change in seasons comes a new direction, a new goal and a new purpose in My Kingdom. Seeming defeat is the birthplace and foundation for victory, My kind of victory. Be not dismayed, but stand tall in the blessing and Glory of My acceptance and love, and watch Me take the ball and bring forth victory from seeming defeat. For does My Word not say the seed must die before it can be raised to glorious life, life abundant, everlasting, and free. Be not dismayed, but stay close to My heart and watch Me work.

See, the joy of the Lord is your strength, strength made manifest through the trials of life. Stay strong, My child, strong against the forces of evil that would try to destroy you, for My way for you is perilous, but filled with My Glory and love. Lay hold of My strength, song, and faithfulness. Step forward unafraid and filled with faith for each day, for many are the pitfalls, but My hand of mercy shall lift you over the pitfalls and cause you to stand, rejoice, and see the victory and salvation of your Lord. Let Me show you when to stand and when to move and how to overcome the wiles of the enemy. The storms have blown, but My grace is stronger and mighty is My love to cause you to grow, expand, and bring forth My plans to bring blessing beyond your understanding. Hold on tight, for the ride is arduous, but you shall rejoice as you see My plan come into focus.

Day 40

Peace, peace, wonderful peace, coming down from the Father above. Stand strong in My peace and keep the light burning of praise. Sacrifice one and you sacrifice the other. Enter into My peace through the avenue of praise. See, it is a sure way into My Presence. Understand and comprehend this truth with steadfastness, for it is a light unto your feet. Relinquish it not and let not the flame be extinguished. Go forth strong in the foundation of My truth and My love. The peace of the Lord is your strength. It comes down upon you as a magnificent blanket of purity to wash away the contaminants of the world.

Now, go forth, My child, under the strength of My protection, showing forth the magnitude of My love and support toward you. Magnify My Name to the four corners of the world and say to your heart, "Peace, be still." Joy comes forth as the morning sun over the mountains, filled with expectation for the new day. Release the heaviness that has built up. Burdens, be gone. Trust and truth say, "There are no burdens. They are the Lord's." So shall it be. Release unto Me all the by-products of those burdens, weariness, trials, tribulations, joyless-ness, sorrow, and despair. Sense My Presence, child, and know its power. Come through the gates with singing and into My courts with praise. Serve your Lord with gladness, thanksgiving, and lightness of heart. Once again be My peacemaker and joy-giver. Let the world major in distraction and destruction, but you major in trust and love, praise and fullness of joy.

A stalemate is broken by the implementation of My Word. Hesitate not to incorporate My words into your heart and understanding, to bring forth peace, tranquility, and an ability to bounce back with agility. Reestablish lines of communication and see stress recede into the background. Blame not! Succeed in areas of distress by concentrat-ing on Me and leaving to Me the results. Fortitude shall bring forth rec-titude. Be on your guard against inappropriate sorrow. Godly sorrow brings forth change through intercession.

Set a standard for life. Set a standard for love (unconditional). Set a standard for peace (a peace unruffled by circumstances). Set a standard for joy (My radiance brought forth by My Presence). Set a standard for wisdom (brought forth through the guidance of My Spirit). Set a stan-dard for life brought forth through communion with Me!

(*I see a lake teaming with fish. Lord, please explain the parable.*) The fish are My blessings jumping out at you with joy and freedom. The lake is you, your life. Your life is filled with blessings, jumping with joy, freedom, and abundance. Join in the joy, freedom, and abundance and know that all is within My timetable and care. Be still and know that I am God and am the rewarder of those who diligently seek Me. Stand fast upon My Word and rejoice in the fulfillment of that Word.

Day 41

Circumstances are moments in time. Don't let them control whole segments of time in your thought life. Give others grace as I give you grace. Stealing from yesterday (pulling along yesterday's circumstances) wreaks havoc with today. Grace is given for today's circumstances, not yesterday's. Leave yesterday behind and live today unhindered by yesterday and unencumbered by tomorrow. There is only grace for today and its blessings. That is how you can love each person you come in contact with unreservedly. Leave the past behind and live totally in the present, rejoicing in the blessings and benefits therein. Cancel old debts and mark them paid!

Study to show yourself approved, a workman who needs not be ashamed (see 2 Tim. 2:15). Steady plodding brings success and firmly shall your feet be planted, one by one. Discover the nuances and intricacies of My Kingdom by acute listening and watching. See My hand in every situation. Truth is your friend and protector. Fear not, but continue to march forth undaunted and unafraid, gleaning truth from the north, south, east, and west. Keep watch upon your mouth to speak truth in love, compassion, and forbearance, void of guile, resentment, or bitterness. Speak the positive in truth and love. Leave the negatives unspoken.

Grace to stand! I have given you grace to stand. The purposes of My heart shall come to pass and the peril shall pass. Green pastures shall become evident and pleasure shall replace pathos. Stand and see the salvation of your Lord and King. Rejoice now!

Strong and sturdy I have made you, able to bear up under the constant barrage that threatened to undo you. Should you say, "My God has forsaken me?" "No," I say to you! Go forth unafraid and able to say, "My God reigns! Nothing can get past His ability to bring victory!" Stand fast! Stand firm and stand strong! Say to the mountain, "Be cast into the sea!" Say to your heart, "The victory is the Lord's!"

Don't be afraid of men's faces or their intimidating words or thoughts. Words of contention, distrust, and disrespect shall always be there, but they need no longer distract you or cause you pain. Confidence in Me is the key, and the knowledge of My love and confidence in you. Many times you shall hear words that would have stopped you in your tracks before and caused agony and pain, but now those same words shall be brushed aside, and you shall refuse to behold them. You shall go forth and forward as I lead, in the confidence, power, and authority of your God!

Walk in the Freedom
of My Love

*Stand fast therefore in the liberty
by which Christ has made us free,
and do not be entangled again
with a yoke of bondage*
(Galatians 5:1).

Day 42

The fulfillment has come slowly, here a piece, there a piece, but now it shall come quickly and you shall marvel at the magnitude of My plans for you. Be not ashamed of the slow progress in the past, for upon it has been built a firm foundation, but rejoice in the soon coming crest of the fulfillment of My promises. Sighing is for a season, but joy comes in the morning. A way has been set to bring to an end the uncertainty and problems of the past. Watch and see My hand at work on your behalf. Dance and sing in the Presence of your King. The clouds shall blow away and the skies shall be blue and radiate forth completion by My Spirit.

The race goes well for the strong of heart. Make sure your heart is strong. Resilience still brings forth the most strength and stamina, for resilience is a guard against injury. Minister love and acceptance. Let go of critical judgments. Speak the positive, word that builds and creates. Leave behind the critical word that causes others to balk and protect the status quo. It may seem like creative criticism to show the way, but it blocks the way. Simply speak the positive, uplifting truth in love that creates and causes miracles to take place. Don't make comparisons. Be My light bearer. A light bearer does not make judgments, does not criticize. A light bearer brings forth light and radiates that light with joy, enthusiasm, and love. Seasoned veterans and seasoned warriors call forth light. My light shall overcome the darkness!

Press forward toward the mark. The way is clear before you. Hurry not. One step at a time is sufficient. Perceive and recognize that I am the door opener. You shall arrive on time. When the winds blow, be at peace. Milestones have been met and passed. Much ground has been traversed. Now, be affirmed and go on. The winds of adversity have blown, but they have left in their wake the seeds of hope and life.

"Eni meni mini mo. Which direction should I go? Should I go here? Should I go there? Wherever should I go?" Heed not the multitude of voices that pull you here and pull you there. Their only purpose is to bring confusion. What are the words spoken by My Spirit? Heed these words of faith, strength, and direction. Words here and words there, unmarked by My Spirit of truth tear about your resolve to stand and be faithful to the commands of your Lord and Savior. Mark these words well, and then stand with determination to finish the course with distinction.

Be not afraid of the long haul. The long haul brings with it added distinction and fulfillment of dreams come true. Renew your sails. Take on new provisions for the trip and set sail once more with new determination to finish it to the end with faithfulness and longsuffering, but most of all with love, compassion, and the sweet victory of success. Time enough for understanding and fulfillment. Now is the time for determined resilience brought forth by praise and righteousness.

Day 43

Ride, freely glide upon this free-flowing ride of life. Progress flows easily within the confines of My love. Pass under bridges, flow through open countryside. And then as darkness falls, continue to flow unrestricted and unafraid, for I am there. I am your boat. Be not affected by the fears of fellow travelers. You rest in Me. You be at peace and enjoy the ride.

Gingerly you have stepped out in My Spirit. Now I will you to step out boldly, seeking My face at every turn, marking each day as an opportunity to minister My love, My word, and My grace to My people. The time has arrived to see, hear, and make known My heart and My ways, to make a way of escape for those who are trapped within the terrifying darkness of the soul and heart. Meaning and hope shall draw them to Me when dissertation and facts could not.

A covenant I make with you this day. You have searched for Me and you have found Me. You have made of your heart a resting place for My peace and My joy. Now I say unto you, "I shall go before you to bring you into new realms of My Glory, righteousness, and right standing with Me." Count the long days of leanness as a sacrifice unto Me, for you have remained faithful. Now I shall lengthen your days and bring forth fatness to your spirit, an overflowing to bring forth My will in your life. (*It has been a sacrifice of obedience, Lord?*) Yea, that I might try and test you to bring forth My best in you. Look not back to the lean years. Look ahead to My Glory. Seek to walk in My Glory. The doors shall open with astounding precision and you shall walk through them jubilantly. Get ready. We shall walk through together, unrestrained. My Spirit shall draw forth from you all that I have promised, for My heart of love has deposited it within you for this day. So rejoice, little one, and know the fulfillment from My heart of love.

Settled in your mind's eye are the avenues of defeat and the avenues of victory and life. Victory comes through the speaking forth of the truth of My words in love. When one speaks through love, it brings life. When one speaks through hurt, it brings death. Minister kindness. Minister longsuffering. Minister an abundance of grace. See My ministering angels bring forth peace where there is no peace, warmth where there is no warmth, and compassion where it has waned. Forbearance is still a virtue to be pursued.

Strength, love, and compassion come forth unabated when one rests in the comfort of My hand. Rest assured, My child, that the perils, worries, and concerns shall all fall away as you rest in the freedom of My love. Stretched you have been, but the ultimate goal is freedom within My love, not freedom within the love of others. The love and acceptance of others is not the goal. The goal is the freedom of understanding and acceptance of the fullness of My love in your life. How others receive and show love is not your problem. You seek Me and receive My freshness daily. How they seek, give, and receive is between Me and them. Release, release, release! Shake off the burdens, restraints, and offenses of others. They are not yours to bear.

Freedom is a state of grace, grace to be unencumbered by what you see and hear. What does My truth say? My grace is sufficient! What does My love say? You are complete in Me! Ride the winds of adversity with confidence and cheer and let Me bear the burdens. Yours is still to see, and in seeing rejoice, for victory is walking in the freedom of My love.

My Will Be Done

Your kingdom come.
Your will be done
on earth as it is in heaven
(Matthew 6:10).

Day 44

Compliance, saying "yes" to My ways, brings life. Saying "yes" to everything brings death. This you have seen. Throughout history, those who have learned to serve Me well have learned to say "no." Say "no" to condemnation, manipulation, fear, doubt, and misuse of time. You manage your time. Don't let others manage it for you. Mismanagement is sin, for it eliminates time spent with Me. Many times, saying "yes" to people is saying "no" to time with Me, and saying "yes" becomes idolatry. Say "yes" to time spent with Me. Say "no" to outside pressures. Where is your focus, on Me or the passing scene? Witness a change in your life as you move from a blanket "yes" to "Thy will be done."

Service is broken down into four categories.

1. Service under grace. Learning to abide under the shadow of My wings.

2. Service to obedience. Learning to hear and to obey My voice.

3. Service to steadfastness. Learning to abide in the face of trial.

4. Service to the King. Walking in victory. Preparing the way of the Lord!

Have you not seen each step come forth? (*Yes, Lord.*) Step forth proudly in the service of your King. Years of struggle and service have served to bring forth steadfastness and trust. Does My Word not said, "Many are the trials of the righteous, but the Lord delivers them from them all"? (See Psalm 34:19.) Step forth proudly in the service of your King and together we shall see victory after victory!

Steadfastness is its own reward, for it brings forth a steadiness, a reliance upon My faithfulness. Faithfulness never fails. It brings forth the fruit sown. Be faithful to My Word in you. See it through to its completion and fulfillment. March forth undaunted by the passing scene. My

Word shall come forth at its appointed time. Seek only to be immersed in My sea of love and in My Presence. Seek to know Me!

Be a pliable twig in My hands and I shall mold you into an arrow that shall always find its mark. Relax in My Presence and feel confident in My love. Traumas shall come and go, but My love shall sustain you in all areas of your life. Complaining prolongs the agony. Complain and strain. Love and draw peace from above. Make melody in your heart and you will always have a brand-new start. Nothing will be able to draw you apart from My absolute authority and stability in your life. Confusion reigns when doubt becomes unrestrained. Believe My Word! Singleness of heart, focusing your mind and heart on Me!

Continue on with confidence and a willingness to accept where others have rejected. Extend the hand of fellowship, not holding account of wrongs or slights. Withholding is harder than giving, for My Spirit within you reaches out with love. Seeming slights shall fade away and peace and calm shall return.

Day 45

Speak to Me your worries and concerns. Stand tall, erect, and confident of My respect and love for you. Showers of blessings shall be revealed to you and you shall understand your calling from Me. Stand still until I release you to move. Consecration is first.

Trials lie ahead, but they shall be fashioned by My hand, so fear not but rejoice in the God of your salvation. Let this faith be in you that overcomes the world. Safe and secure you shall be as you seek My face and speak forth My words to set the captives free. Surefooted strength is My gift to you brought forth from the furnace of affliction.

Faith and circumstances work together to create wholeness and a disciplined life complete in everything. The scales over the eyes shall fall away and the truth of My Word shall ring forth and bring victory and freedom. Look for My Word to come to fulfillment and look for

My love to conquer all. Sound judgment and fierce loyalty shall be My gift to you.

Allow Me to mold, to shape, and to form from the inside out, creating life and a way in the wilderness for you and for those who follow you. Maintain a quiet diligence to remain pliable and able to remain at peace in the midst of the storm. Conform to My Spirit, not to the passing scene. Stand convinced of My power to change, to mold, and to shape, and you shall see miracles come forth.

Stand back and watch Me work. Watch the canvas take shape and form with color and vibrancy. The pieces of the puzzle are coming together to make a beautiful picture for others to gaze upon and see the beauty of God. Short-term blessings bring about long-term blessings and victories. Cultivate vision. (*How do I do that, Lord?*) By seeing what I show you and implementing it into the big picture. Vision brings structure and structure brings strength. See, and seeing, believe.

Surely I have said that the fullness shall come and the windows of Heaven shall pour forth My wisdom, compassion, and understanding upon you, that the blind shall see and lame shall walk and those who walk in darkness shall see the light and come into its warmth. The time of My visitation draws nigh and the wholeness that you search for shall completely and marvelously transform and complete you into My likeness. For now, rest in the hope and continue to come forth in peace, serenity, and the ability to love and rejoice in the smallest of steps. Have I not said, "You are My songbird to proclaim My love and compassion upon My people?" The time draws forth and you shall see Me. Be as that singing bird that meets the dawn of each new day with a song of joy. Draw from Me that which you need for the day and see Me draw from you depths that you know not of. Linger longer and know Me!

Many times I have said unto you, "Let not your heart be troubled." Listen once again to the strains of the Word, "Let not your heart be troubled." Let your heart rest within the confines of My love, listening not to outside babblings, but hearing and seeing My Word and relying on My truth. Contend not with conflicting reports but stand firm in My love and let Me make the moves, content to watch and wait. Resist not the tides as they ebb and flow, but know that the ebb and flow shall form boundaries of beauty. Stand in My love. Release it all unto Me and rejoice.

Day 46

Stake your claim and stick with it. The stakes are high and the sacrifice has been great, but the rewards are even greater. Mountains have been crossed, valleys forged, but I say to you, you shall dance and sing and triumph in the Presence of your God. The walls shall come tumbling down and the victory shall be to God's people. Forge ahead, looking not back, but looking ahead to the promise, singing the songs of Zion. A new day is dawning with all its fullness therein. Glory in the highest!

The house of the Spirit is built on a strong foundation of truth and is established in the fire of adversity. Marginal areas line up and become established as the fire burns away the dross. Ultimately, what stands is pure gold. Hesitate not to withstand, through patience, the fire and oppressive winds that blow. But see, through it all, My strong hands of love, holding you steady and providing the leadership you need to help you prevail and continue forward. Strong and mighty winds have blown, but the outcome is sure. The strength obtained is immeasurable. Stand strong, My child.

The depths of the soul are tilled by deeper fellowship with Me. To know Me, one must stay in constant, not sporadic, fellowship with Me. Contained within the human heart is the ability to know Me and walk in constant fellowship, but few do. Constant awareness is the key. It opens the door to communion, sweet communion, with your Maker and Friend. See, the door is wide open. Walk and talk with Me, and discover vistas unknown to you through precious fellowship with Me. The door is open. Walk through!

Seek and you shall find. Knock, and the door shall be opened to you. Abide under the shadow of My wings. Patience has caused My Spirit to flourish within you. The ballast has been cut and you shall begin to rise to be carried along by My Spirit. I have charted a course by which you shall travel. The scenery shall be breathtakingly beautiful, and you shall partake of the miraculous along the way. Maintain your balance through constant prayer. See, it shall become a way of life, and together we shall see the pieces of the puzzle come together as a beautiful picture.

Day 47

Leave the hurt behind like old clothes that do not fit. Size up the situation, forgive, and go on. Reach into My heart and grasp My kind of love. Earnestly remember, My love is your highest calling. You are beginning to grasp the essence of it all, love given for its own sake, not for its return. To give that sort of love you must be secure in My love. Continue to follow it through. The rewards are great. Stand secure in My love and watch the mountains fall. Continue to nibble the fragrant grasses in the valley of the shadow of death, for I am with you. My rod and My staff are guiding you and you shall live in the house of the Lord forevermore.

Stand clear, stand out of the way and watch My hand of blessing fall upon you and the torrent of blessing shall flow, as down through a valley, unabated. Stand aside and watch it flow and bring refreshing newness and life. Restored, restored you shall be, free to receive from Me all that you have believed and watched for. The gifts are in the residue of the flood. Resist the temptation to reach ahead too soon. Let Me bring to you people, places, and things to establish your way. All shall be in order and solidly placed. Watch in anticipation and blessed assurance.

See Me in everything, the beauty of the simple to the most complex. Register all that I bring your way and weigh it in the balance of My love. See the need and be My spokesman. Respond within the guidelines of My Word to you. See and be the fulfillment of My Word. The heavens respond with the Glory of My perfection in you. Be refreshed and respond with the freshness of My Holy Spirit. You shall be retrieved and restored. Fear not, for the results are sure.

A mighty wind has blown through your house, forcing the doors of hiding to be opened that the prisoner might be set free. Worship your God in faithfulness and truth, and let truth be spoken in your inner man. Sinister forces have kept you locked away for years. Now the light of My love has burst through that you might rejoice in the light of freedom and strength, forever freed from the stranglehold of fear. Now sing in joy, strength, and healing, knowing the magnitude of My healing power and love. So be it! Your loving Father! Amen!

The Sky Is the Limit

With God all things are possible
(Matthew 19:26).

Day 48

The gates are opened wide. Receive! Vast areas of darkness and light have been revealed to you. Test the waters as you walk. Does your spirit expand and revel in the beauty and expectancy, or is it repelled by the darkness and sense of ominousness that permeates? See My light shining in the darkness and let Me reveal to you My Word and direction. See Me move in your life with rapidity and strength of purpose. Strength of purpose is your song evermore, brought about by pain.

Cease your struggles. Let Me show you the magnitude of My plan for you, detail by detail. Released and restored you are becoming. I have sustained you and upheld you in the midst of many trials. I have made My Son to shine upon you in power and in truth. Now the truth of My words throughout the years shall ring in your ears and cause you joy.

Stand firm, My child, in the solid foundation of My love and freedom. You have walked many a weary mile. Now stand firm and rejoice in the sure power of My promises to you. The flood tide of the enemy has ravished, but the flood tide of My Spirit shall restore and make new. Stand, My child! Stand and rejoice in the fulfillment of My Word!

See into the future. See the beginning of miracles and events in your life that shall transform you and all that you know. See Me bringing forth in you stamina and a multitude of miraculous events to mold and shape your life. Constant change shall enrich and bring forth all that I have for you. The sky is the limit. You shall be the bearer of Good News that shall bring joy to the people of God and bring release to the captives. Rejoice and see that day fast arriving. The magnitude of it shall astound you. Be at peace, for the fulfillment is sure.

Open your heart to receive more of Me. Feed on the Word of My Spirit. Richly feed and be restored. Capture what is Me. Can the eaglet fly without food? No, he would waste away. So shall you find nourishment for your soul day by day. I have determined the stars. I have set each day in order for you.

Gingerly you have marked each day by My Spirit, hoping to find peace and joy therein. Now I say, "Stake your claim each day knowing that My Spirit waits to proclaim the Glory of that day. Partake each day of the blessings therein, resplendent with the joys of My love. Release unto Me all fears for the future and run with Me with unbounded joy and freedom. Be released from the burdens of the past and soar."

Sheltered you have been. Restrained and held back from the fray of life, that you not be destroyed. Many have tasted of freedom and come up short, lacking the vision to make it work. Freedom demands much wisdom and discernment. It knows the difference between trouble and pleasure. It sees clearly and resolves to rejoice in the seeing. It measures all things against truth and knows the correct balance. Freedom takes time to see, and yet seeing to believe. Time it has taken. Chomp not at the bit, but allow Me to slowly acquaint you with freedom, freedom that brings alive and brings hope to the heart. Many shall know of this freedom and in seeing, believe. Carry on with faith. Stand firm. Your day is soon arriving and all shall be revealed for you to see and know the salvation of your God. The heavens ring with joy. The joy of your salvation comes forth.

Day 49

Landmarks are being approached and passed and much ground traversed quickly. Struggle not with the hardships along the way. They too will be passed quickly. Keep your eyes on the promises and rejoice and be glad, for My Spirit goes with you to encourage and lift up. Lift up your heart and rejoice this day for the awareness of My Presence shall increase and be as a constant companion of peace and contentment.

Your walk shall become like being on a skateboard. It glides in and out of situations and maneuvers well. It is quick and smooth. Take this time to rest and reflect, refresh and restore. Listen with clarity and come often to the well. Say with assurance, "All is well with My soul." Concern shall be replaced with joy. Sweep away the cobwebs of your heart. The sticky cobwebs of self-pity, fear, and doubt keep you immobile. Listen to your heart. Say with assurance, "The blessings of the Lord are upon Me to bring me into a broad place of peace and security in His love. Hallelujah!"

A standard bearer you are, out in the wilderness, calling in the wandering ones with no anchor of hope. Seek to know Me in new ways of strength, brought forth by endurance. The way has been arduous but My Spirit has stabilized, comforted and led. Now sing My songs of deliverance and see deliverance dwell within you, for it will find a place reserved within you to dwell. Seek not to rescue the aimless wanderer. Seek instead to show the way of deliverance within the shelter of My wings, for the ways of life bring sorrow and pain, but the ways of My Spirit bring deliverance, peace, love, and joy. Stand on that promise with hope and endurance for you shall yet see My face of provision. Seek to know Me, and I shall make My heart known through you!

First and foremost, to thine own God be true. The track is littered with those who have started but not completed the journey with victory and distinction. Continue on with the wealth of provision I have given you for the trip—strength of character and determination.

The winds of pain have blown in all directions, weeding out the chaff. Stamina of heart and spirit it has taken to maintain balance. Transference of stamina shall take place not many days hence, restoring balance to the physical. Seasons of change shall abound, requiring strength to accomplish all that shall be set before you.

See the light of My smile upon you. Let it shine to bring forth warmth, love, and newness of life. I have brought you forth to a broad place, a place of restoration and contentment. I shall lead you in ways you have not known. The signposts along the way, big and bright. Let Me show you vistas, by My Spirit, that shall thrill your heart and bring you into a broader place of service and contentment. The days of struggle and meandering are coming to an end, making way for a greater day of enlightenment and joy. The scales have tipped. Hold on tight for the change has begun, safe harbor reached. Truth has won out. The truth of My Word to you proclaimed year after year has set the enemy on his ear! Your way shall be made clear and you shall hear and not fear. Simply say, "God's truth says…"

Day 50

Your times and seasons have always been in My hands and shall continue to be. The trials and tribulations have proven your faith and brought a strength available in no other way. I have tried you and proven you as pure gold, fit for the Master's use. Restraints have been broken. Lessons of mighty magnitude have been learned. Mount up as on eagles' wings and survey the world that I have fashioned for you. Stay sweet and pliable through the oil of My Spirit of love. Remain stable by My inner sustaining power that transforms and glows from within. Secured you have been and secured you shall be, standing on the Rock who has been your fortress and your shield.

Stand forth as an illustration of My faithfulness and an illustration of My inheritance. Favor I have bestowed upon you in the past, and favor shall fall upon you in the present and future. Trust Me to bring forth the right result. Be not ashamed, but stand tall and proud of who I am in you. You are a walking symbol of My grace. You are not alone. Singleness of heart I have given to you as a gift. It shall carry you through unscathed. Be at peace and respond with love.

Now you can truly say, "Sticks and stones may break my bones but words will never hurt me," for you have faced into the wind and come up strong. The weight of the world has fallen from your shoulders that you might fly with freedom, restored by the might of My power and love. You have turned a corner, walking in My love. It shall bring forth added truth and sustenance for your soul and spirit. Fear not for the length of your days. Fear not for the content. Now go forth with a song in your heart and a song of praise on your lips, for My Word has prevailed and a new season of life has begun, a fruitful season.

My Love Will Carry You Through

Because he has set his love upon Me,
therefore I will deliver him; I will set him on high,
because he has known My name.
He shall call upon Me, and I will answer him;
I will be with him in trouble;
I will deliver him and honor him

(Psalm 91:14-15).

Day 51

Sanctification is a painful struggle, but it brings forth fruit immeasurable. Let the peace of God reign in your heart this day. Let heart peace invade your soul and show you the way to contentment. Contentment in whatever circumstance is great gain. Be enmeshed in My love and removed from the noise and confusion of the rocket's great blare around you. Seeking to know Me is the excellent way. Continue on in your quest and know that I will be there to answer your request. The heavens resound with joy at the strengthening of one who seeks. Go forth unencumbered by doubt. Raise your voice in praise and be assured of this very thing: My love will carry you through.

(*Holy Spirit, thank You for teaching me a new way of reading Your word, praying the Scriptures back to You as a prayer.*) It will become a way of life, restoring what has been stolen and recapturing that which has been polluted, bringing healing. Rejoice, for you shall continue to be restored and renewed in the beauty of holiness and you shall recapture the joy of your first love.

Constrain not, simply lift up love and comfort, bringing to light inequities. The light of My smile shall shine brighter, and you shall see progress. Be not concerned, for My arm of righteousness shall prevail and bring forth peace and joy. Shrink not from the oncoming tide but stand strong and steady, revealing My Spirit within you to sustain and bring life. Time and again you shall see miracles flow from you to declare My marvelous acts. Rejoice and be glad, for the time is upon you to bring forth that for which you ask, My Spirit of comfort and love given forth to bless. The tide has truly changed, bringing forth abundance, truth, and faithfulness. Sit amazed but not confounded, and the God of peace shall establish and bring you joy.

Stand fast, firmly planted in the sound word of righteousness impressed upon your heart by the Spirit of God, steadfast in the knowledge of My love and faithfulness. Let not up your stance of faith and sound doctrine. The true test of servanthood is the ability and desire to survive, that one might live to serve again in a greater capacity and magnitude, not tainted from the past, but free to move ahead un-encumbered by the past. Step forth into the future free to move, live, and have your being, in the strength, purity, and freedom of My love, secure in the knowledge of who I have created you to be. Now unto Him who has provided all that you need, be Glory forever!

My strength I have put within you. Think not that you are weak, for strength of character and purpose have spurred you on with singleness of heart and mind to bring forth those things that have been placed in your heart by My Spirit of love and grace. Continue on, unruffled by outside circumstances, confident in the outcome, and serenely confident in My love and the fulfillment that I am bringing forth. Continue to stand fast in the firm and sustaining power of My plan for you.

Day 52

Seeds of righteousness sprout and grow in the incubator of struggle. They bring forth fruit of strength, fortitude, and the impenetrable power to stand in the face of evil, allowing God's victory to prevail. You have stood. You have prevailed. You have remained steady in the face of apparent destruction. But know this, My child, the tide of the enemy shall not prevail, for I have placed My anointing upon you and My cloak of righteousness surrounds you, My angels protect you and you shall yet see the fulfillment of all that I have put before you. See, My child, the night does become day and all that has brought agony and pain shall be brushed away and the dawning of the new day shall bring joy to your heart. So rise and be healed to the Glory of God your Father, and the light of My countenance shall shine about you and bring you peace!

The steps of a righteous man are ordered by the Lord that his life might shine forth the radiance of God. Light and darkness are alike to Me. I work in both and bring forth My attributes in the midst of trials and in the sunniest of days. Fear not the times of pain but stand strong in My Presence, redeeming the time with joy and anticipation, drawn forth from faith and hope in Me. You shall see results far beyond your ability to see and expect, for I have placed within you patience and hope which will not be blotted out, but shall come forth in victory and song. Remain in My love and prevail.

Can you not see, My Spirit is upon you and brings you forth to do My Will. You shall sound forth the alarm to those languishing on the sidelines, bringing them forth into the new day of service and prosperity of spirit. It is a new day being formed from the dust of shattered lives, bringing forth the promises that I have spoken to them for years. They have seen My hand of mercy upon them and yet have languished on the sidelines for lack of nourishing. Be not afraid to speak forth, for I shall lead you and let you know how, where, and when. All you have experienced shall become the platform upon which you stand, for you have experienced fully the pain and agony so well-known to many who need a touch from Me. You can empathize with your heart and yet unwaveringly lead them straight to Me to be rescued and saved. Struggle not with the details but leave them to Me. It will come about naturally and will be a joy to your heart. You are My precious child and I can use you to proclaim My goodness and steadfastness. Lean not to your own understanding. Relax in My arms and commit your ways to Me and together we shall see the horror in people's lives changed to love, peace, prosperity, and joy.

Lessons learned have a lasting quality about them that redeem other areas of life and bring refreshment and stability. You are My child in whom I am well-pleased. Place not your confidence in people, places, and things, but place your confidence in My ability to come forth in you and to handle all circumstances to bring victory and My way for you. You have believed it in the past. Believe it now. Take counsel, but bring it to Me before you act on it.

Day 53

Appearing and being are two separate things. Be what you appear. Be not afraid to be what I have created you to be. Compromise is not necessary to appear to be as others. Stand your ground and appear to be as you are. Only truth is stable and a foundation on which to build. All else flops in the wind and leaves others uneasy, including yourself. Standards are to be upheld with judgment. Be true to you. Don't allow other's lowered standards to put your standards into subjection. I will honor you, even if they do not. Is that not better anyway? You are a standard bearer. Bear that standard with pride in Me. Do not allow your standard to be subdued under other's standards. Relinquish not your placement by Me as a standard bearer. Stand true to your calling and I will stand true to you. I, you, and your calling are one, a standard bearer of the truth!

Life is like a circus. Many rings performing at the same time in each life. Each is capable of destruction and death without My intervening hand of protection. Wild animals that are dangerous, yet subdued are kept under control by the trainer. High-wire acts take strength, courage, and precision, which is like life. Clowns bring joy, laughter, and levity in the midst of such intensity. And beautiful costumes bring beauty to the proceedings. There is much going on in your life that defies reason, but I am the Leader of all that transpires, and you can be at peace with confidence. Know that every area of your life will be played with precision to know the completed show will be one of beauty, perfection, and precision. Rest in that assurance.

I have seen your plight and have calmed the raging waves, and brought to you the ability to stand in the midst of trial. I have paved your way with My Spirit of praise. Take full advantage of this precious gift by calling it into being at every opportunity, for it brings with it the gift of prosperity and achievement, and it opens the door to victory. Shun all forms of corruptive speech (complaining and criticizing), for it is the opposite of praise. In this way you will continue to see change and victory.

Release unto Me your fears and reservations that we might move on from the desert to the oasis. Stand tall and resolute in My presence, for you are My beloved child in whom I am well-pleased. Look not back to the past but stand resolved and at peace in the present, released from the struggles and trials of the past. Relax and enjoy the view. The stillness will give way to raucous times of endeavor. But I am with you in the stillness and I am with you in the noise. I will bless you in the stillness and I will bless you in the times of activity. It is a time of forgiveness and the laying down of strife to bring forth a new day of peace. Many will not lay down the strife and remain where they are, locked into time and space. Go forward without malice or fear, knowing that I have calmed the waters and brought forth peace. Accept each for what they can give and go on. Do not demand that they realize what they have done. Simply accept and go on. I know each and every detail. I know and see and that is all that is necessary. Loosed to be a blessing. You are loosed to be a blessing, lifted above the mire and ready to soar. Lift up your heart and rejoice and be among My saints who shout, "Glory in the highest, peace on earth!"

Day 54

Cherish this time with Me. It will be like none other. I will speak to you in the day, and I will speak to you in the night hours. Our time together shall be precious and well-spent. Let Me direct your days, detail by detail. The enemy will try to get in, but he cannot. My power is greater, and you shall be aware of My Presence moment by moment, day by day. Cease your striving and come into peace with Me. You've come a long way, and the best is yet to come.

See, the sun is shining. See to it that the Son always shines in your life through joy and song. In times of trouble, in the midst of the storm, My light shines even brighter in one's life. Seeds of trouble are sown and the crop seems to come forth in abundance. But in the midst are My strong plants of righteousness which shall come forth bearing much fruit. I have made you to be My gatherer of grapes. Be not afraid to gather, but remember, you are gathering for Me, not for you. They are not to circle around you but around Me. Go forth with singing and hope bubbling up in your heart, for I have made this day for you to enjoy.

Test your wings today. Fly high. Concentrate on Me and see that you will catch the high currents. Be in My Presence all day and let Me begin to soothe and heal your inner being, the inner child that stands back and weeps. Be not concerned, simply be and I shall direct your paths. You shall seek Me and know Me in ways you know not of. I have made you to worship Me. Sing forth your praises with abandon, with no fear, for I am with you and together there is nothing we cannot conquer.

It is a day of rest with redemptive value. Rest from worries and cares. Rest in My arms. Lean back and let Me hold the weight. I am your Husband and Father. I perform both rolls and will bring you into a high place of serenity and peace. Rejoice, My child, and be glad, for you have faced the enemy and have prevailed. He has not overcome you, but you have stood to My Glory. Rest is imperative. Rest in body, soul, and spirit. Fear not that it won't get done, for it will in My time and in My way. Measure the need and respond as I lead. I give My beloved rest. The way is clear and moving forward in My timing and at My bidding.

Life doesn't always follow the way you think, but there is always a purpose and a reason. My Spirit is always enveloping you and carrying you forward. I have strengthened you, and I will continue to lead you beside streams of living water. The strain and stress of life shall be transformed into the newness that you have so desired. Relax, let Me fill you, refine and polish you for your Master's purposes. Stand ready to march forward with resilience and power in My Name, armed with My Spirit of praise, released from the fetters that bind, and amazed at the bright future I have for you.

The seasons of change have worked their weight in gold, filled, polished, and prepared. The changes shall continue to come to you with rapidity. My Spirit hovers over you and is preparing and charging you for the work at hand. Relish My closeness! Be released from all doubt and fear, for the path ahead is filled with light and My Presence. Drink in My freshness. Shine forth My radiance. Be once more that beacon of Mine to draw the lost to My light and warmth. Praise begets praise. Light restores light. I send you forth to restore and beget by the power of My Spirit. Pour out My Spirit upon My people. Lavish it upon them with gentleness and song, lightness and fun. I have strengthened you, empowered you, and send you forth, knowing who you are in Me.

Day 55

Stand firm. Do not be swayed by buffeting of any kind. Stand your guard and express your ability to see clearly. The scene is changing. I am bringing you into a beautiful open plane. Don't be afraid to bask in the beauty and wonderment of it. My hand is upon you to cause you to flourish and grow. You have been sustained. Now we shall go on to flourishing. The pieces shall begin to fit together, and you shall see a beautiful picture begin to form from the chaos. My power to bring it forth is with you, and you shall see mighty miracles by My hand. Go forth this day in joy, for neither fire nor flood have swayed you, and the sunshine and beauty of My Kingdom shall bring healing and restore unto you the sense of peace and well-being that is your inheritance.

Stir up the fires, the flame of My Spirit within you. Let the warmth of My love wash over you and be refreshed in the knowledge of My loving care. Have you not seen My hand of protection and the miracles I have wrought in your behalf? The story has not been half told. Surely it has not begun, for the times and the seasons await you, and the trials that have beset you shall give way to abundant freedom and joy. The day awaits in the beauty and splendor of My holiness. A way has been made and My Spirit hovers to bring it forth. Go forth this day in the Spirit of faithfulness and uprightness, and together we shall see the Jordan part and the victory won. See Me in the blowing breezes, in the smallest detail, in the smallest pleasure. See Me in each moment and rejoice.

You are a standard bearer, rising to the occasion each and every day. The stage has been small, but it is growing as each day passes. Strength of purpose has carried you along in a strong current. You are learning as you go. Refreshment of body, soul, and spirit is coming and with it an assessment of all that has transpired. Line upon line, precept upon precept, it all falls together and causes truth to be seen. Rise to the occasion and see the salvation of your King.

My child, listen carefully! Don't let down your guard. Your guard is a singing heart, a rejoicing heart, singing praises to your Father. Such a heart cannot be moved, neither will it be afraid, but it will be like the rushing spring of fresh, cool water dancing in the sunlight. Such have I created you to be. Let Me show you a better way. Let Me show you vistas to delight you and make you glad. Appreciate what I am telling you and go forth this day singing praises and making beautiful music to delight us both.

Liberally bless My people. Swath them with your love, which is My love, and the awareness of My Presence. Let them know that My heart reaches out to them. Out of the ash heap shall rise my phoenix (a beautiful lone bird which lived in the Arabian desert for 500 to 600 years, then consumed by fire rose renewed from the ashes to start another long life). You shall lift Me up with joy and show the way, My way of hope, faithfulness, and the ability to stand, unmoved by the world and outside pressures by hearing My Word and standing. Stand steady, My child, and faint not, but see Me in the midst of all trauma. Start now to rejoice, for the victory is now and you shall see the victory of your God. Go forth with singing and song and a willing heart to take pleasure in Me.

The Storm Is Over

He calms the storm,
so that its waves are still.
Then they are glad because they are quiet;
so He guides them to their desired haven

(Psalm 107:29-30).

Day 56

Leadership is based on the ability to lead My people into the Promised Land, the land flowing with milk and honey which is the Holy of Holies, which is a place of fellowship with Me, a deep intimate relationship with Me. Contrary to popular belief, I am not found in the rushing brook, in the morning sunrise, or the majestic mountain. I am found in the human heart. It is there where I reside in power. It is there where I take the crooked and make it straight and set the captives free. Seek to know Me in a new dimension that shall take you from the valley into the majestic mountain peaks of a walk with Me. The door is open and the vista is limitless. Come! Let us proceed!

Search the Scriptures and know the intricacies of My Word. Let Me point out to you nuances that shall delight your heart and cause you to grow. My Word is truly an open door to you that cannot be closed. Loose yourself from the trials of life through the laying hold of My Word to you. Seek and you shall find. Knock, and the door shall be opened unto you. Yes, a new day has begun and the trials that you have known shall fade away into the distance as the vista of the new day opens before you.

The pages of time are rapidly turning, proclaiming My return. Magnify My Name, and take not unto yourself the Glory of that Name. Reflect My Glory and call it not your own. Relax and be and I will do in your life. March forth in joy, but let Me be the teleprompter. Let Me be the inner glow. Let Me be the force that motivates you from moment to moment. Let Me be the one to give you to the world as a gift—and I will in My time. In the meantime, stay faithful to your calling. Minister My love as never before, for I have called you to love. You shall shine forth My radiance and draw others to Me.

Shower your love on others with no fear of lack of return, for I return double and refill your reservoir to overfilling. In the past, you have looked to others for that refilling and they could not. Only I have the power to refill. Look to Me and give as I lead, as the anointing I give and My Word directs. See your reward in Me, not in others. Be My bond slave. I will reward you openly and without reservation. Go forward this day with the assurance that you can never be hurt again, for your reward does not come from people, your reward comes from Me. The rewards are great to the one who toots not his own horn, but lets Me toot it for him. Lay down your horn. Continue to see Me as your provider in all things. Together, we shall walk new ground and see new vistas of splendor, for more is available when people are no longer your source. Let us proceed.

Day 57

Hold steady. Yield not to the temptation to succumb to hopelessness, for I am your hope. And behold the days shall bring forth signs of hopefulness and I shall rejoice over you. Stand ready to move only at My bidding, for now is a time of preparation. You do not stand alone. My angels are round about you, releasing unto you blessings and honor. Release unto Me your sadness and let Me replace it with gladness. See, I am here. Say to your heart, we shall prevail!

Concentrate on the immediate. Yesterday was yesterday. Today is today. Concentrate on today.

The sands of time shall fall one upon the other and cause you to see the whole picture unmarred by shadows and assumptions. I have cleared the path for you to walk ahead unhindered by bottlenecks or past traumas. Go forth each day rejoicing in that day on its own merits. Rejoice in the appropriation of My love and go forth rejoicing in the completeness of each day.

Stand now in the firm assurance of your place in My beloved, as set forth by Me. No longer shall you wonder if I can cover you and protect you. You shall know, and My Glory shall be revealed through your life in a new and more powerful way. Never again shall you say, "I wonder." You shall say, "I know!" A reservoir of hope has been building in your heart, pushing out the residue of hopelessness and sadness. Look not to the past, for looking to the past brings up the hopelessness of the past. Look to today, for today is bright with the hope and promise of the freedom, power, and blessings from My hand. Rejoice in God, your Maker. Make it a habit to rejoice in the God of your salvation. Be encouraged, My child, and fear not the days as they unfold one by one, for the destination is sure and the results shall make you exclaim with joy, "My God is an awesome God and nothing is too hard for Him!"

Struggle is not necessary, but a willing heart. Cast your cares on Me and let Me carry the burden of your understanding. Be a long distance runner, prepared for the long haul. For I am with you to assure you and strengthen and to cheer you on. You will see changes intensify as your strength returns and you become aware of My very nudges along the way. Study to show yourself approved, a workman who needs not be ashamed. Be faithful in the small things, and I will bless you in the big things. Be not afraid to go forward, undaunted by the past but spurred on by the vision given. It truly is a new day filled with great gain.

The gate has swung wide open for you. Pitch a tent in the wilderness that you can continue to go in and out and minister to the needs of those who are still in the wilderness, hungering and thirsting for the Word of Life that will set them free. You shall show others that there is a way through the wilderness that leads to life, refreshing, and hope. I will show you how to minister hope to a dying people with no hope. You are a picture story and My Spirit is upon you to bring forth My will and abundant life, full and free. Let not your heart be troubled, neither let it be afraid, for My hand of restoration and freedom is upon you, and the reality of My love shall be manifest and made known to you in a new and all inclusive way. In peace you shall drink from the well of restoration. Your soul shall magnify the Lord and recount His mercies to you and you shall see and respond to new ways of moving by My Spirit of truth.

Day 58

A reasonable service has been to stand in the midst of the trial. Now, I say to you, "Rejoice in your heart, My child, for the days of waiting are at an end and the days of life and fulfillment stand ready for you." Seek My face each day to bring forth the fulfillment in your life and in the lives of others. Face into the wind, My child, face into the wind and let it prove you faithful. Your heart is strong to stand. There shall be no lack, for I have promised to be your source and your supply. Stand, My child, in faithfulness and I shall prove Myself faithful. As a priest unto Me, you shall bring them forth unto Me, and I shall heal them and set them free. Line upon line, precept upon precept has brought it forth. Stand strong, My child.

I raise a standard before you. Walk in it. Walk in My ways unflinchingly. Cry aloud saying, "My God is an awesome God. Nothing is too difficult for Him!" You will find within your heart a new openness to respond with love, unfeigned, free to receive without restraint. Laughter comes with freedom. Be free! Stand aside and watch Me work. Say not to yourself, "The weight is to heavy," but say to yourself, "My God is faithful." Go forth this day with a song in your heart and a bounce in your step, for My faithfulness is your life and your song.

(*Lord, help me to love with agape love.*) It's going to be fun, an adventure. See Me place the desire in your heart and be encouraged as you see it come to pass. Stand encouraged. Now is the time to rejoice and go forward in the fullness and radiance of My Spirit. It is truly a new day with new ways. Release unto Me your spirit to soar, for I have given you a spirit of delight and you shall again delight in all that I bring to you and cause that spirit of delight to be birthed in others. Be refreshed, My little one, and continue on in the journey of life with renewed vision and vigor. I love you!

Nothing has been lost during this time. My Word stands in your life forever. Fasten your eyes on Me and proceed. Seek to know My will, for I will not forsake you, but will hold you to My heart and release you from the sadness that has bound you, for it is a new day. Sing, for the night as you have known it to be is over. The day dawns brilliantly, like the light coming over the mountains, and nothing can stay its light, not even the mountains, for the light fills the whole sky. My light is in your heart and shall shine forth with greater strength and brilliance, drawing others to its light. I have opened a way to you through a broad and beautiful valley. Straight and narrow is that path that I have laid out for you, but flooded with My light and My Glory. I have loved you with an everlasting love. Stand on that love. That love gives your life meaning. It directs your paths. Continue to seek to know that love in all its fullness and together we shall give that love unendingly.

Look out over the vastness of all that is before you. It is limitless. See the times and the days, weeks and years are culminating into a time of richness and focused fulfillment and blessing. Continue on in your quest to know My Word and to understand it by the power of My Holy Spirit. The days ahead are rich and full, and full of the knowledge and character of My Word to you and through you. Reach out your heart and mind to drink deeply, and I shall make of you a water fountain of life, abundant life in My Name. Refreshed you shall be and restored, filled with My Glory, peace, faithfulness, and love. See, it comes upon you and transforms you, making of you a servant in whom I am well-pleased. Continue on, My child, and know that the door is open wide and the fulfillment is sure. Strain not to fulfill My dreams in you. Take the land step by step. Now is the time to embark, but rush not. Keep your focus on Me and the rest shall fall into place. Strain not! Stress not! Rejoice in the now!

Day 59

The wages of sin is death. The wages of obedience is eternal life and life abundant. You have chosen life, abundant and free. Stay free. See your choices moment by moment and stay free. Lay down your burdens this day. It truly is a turning point, a day to bring you into the Promised Land of My promises for you. Success is measured by My Spirit of praise within you. Respond with clarity and joy. Sing upon your bed. Sing within and without the confines of your home. Sing with My joy overflowing. Take unto yourself a new awareness of My Presence within your singing, for it is precious to Me. Light the fire of My Spirit within you (praise is the igniter) with magnificent and perpetual praise.

Strong and effective measures have I employed to bring forth My will in you. Strength of purpose have I instilled in you to bring forth My will in this Last Day. Fear not, My little one, for I have not, nor shall I ever abandon you, but I shall bring forth in you and through you beyond your wildest dreams. Search the Scriptures and let Me build within you a fortress of My understanding and the ability to see, understand, and know. Stand straight and tall in My Spirit, lighting the fires of My Spirit wherever you go, for I have prepared, initiated, and brought forth great and mighty wonders for you to perform by My Spirit of praise within you.

Stand back, survey, and forgive. It is a testament of My Spirit residing and acting in you. Daily cleanse your heart of all the built-up debris of the day that it not pile up, surround, and overpower you. Every negative word spoken is evidence of debris retained. Go forth this day, determined to be My clear channel of love, freed from the bondages of self. Lay down your life before Me. See it as a sacrifice unto Me to be broken as bread, to bring forth my perfect will. Minister life to those around you. Build up their hearts and they shall see the Glory of their God.

Listen, My child, and know My heart. Light draws to light. Dark draws to dark. Draw in My light. Stand in that light and drink deeply. The light of My Word overshadows all darkness. Drink deeply and chase away the darkness with My light, My Word. Strength and boldness come forth from that Word. Seek My face with greater diligence and be restored in the light, My Word. Stand in awe at the clarity of My Word in your heart and be at peace as each piece of the puzzle of your life comes into place. Be at peace and proclaim My goodness. Now unto Him who is able to do above all you ask or think be Glory, now and forevermore. Amen and amen!

Be My Ambassador of Love

Since you have purified your souls
in obeying the truth through the Spirit
in sincere love of the brethren,
love one another fervently with a pure heart
(1 Peter 1:22).

Day 60

Release unto Me the cares of this life. My Spirit of praise is upon you. It is the marriage between prophecy and joy. Enter in with all your heart and praise Me with all your might and heart. Revealed unto you shall be My heart. I have placed you in the midst of strangers, but none is a stranger. Reach out in love and let Me pull their heart strings through you. It is the strength of My love through you that shall turn the tide and calm the storms in their lives. Be My ambassador of love without restraint and let them know of My love for them. Be that beacon light of hope to those around you, for I shall send you to My people with a message of hope and encouragement. My love through you shall warm them and point them to Me, their hope and their salvation.

Search the Scriptures and find the truth about My Glory. Treasures await you in the storehouse of My Word. Revealed to you shall be the fullness of My Glory. Seek Me with relish and enthusiasm for the truth revealed, that shall be part of your life and the lives of others. The heavens declare the Glory of God. We shall proceed.

I have made you unique among My people, unique to proclaim My Word, to sing forth My praises, to release the prisoners from bondage and to proclaim the acceptable time of the Lord. For I have set you upon a straight and narrow path, and I have shod your feet with the message of truth, and fortified you with My Word, and have set within your heart a flame that will never waver. Enter into each day with thanksgiving and with song. Enter in with all your heart, for the time is short and the rewards are great.

Now lay down your life before Me for My ways shall be your ways and My words shall be your words. My compassion and love shall be your compassion and love. My wisdom and knowledge shall be the wisdom and knowledge that you shall give forth by the anointing of My Spirit through you. Your hands shall be My hands of healing. Your voice shall ring forth the truth of My heart. You shall hear with My ears and see with My eyes, and your feet shall go where I lead you to go. I shall enlarge your sphere of influence to bring forth My Word in due season, for I have planned and I shall bring forth that plan to delight your heart and fulfill all that I have spoken to your heart. Lay down your pride of ownership, for I shall exchange it for a pride in Me. My heart rejoices over you. Be lifted up and confident of this very thing, that He who has begun a good work in you shall complete it to the Glory of God.

Day 61

Lasting fruit is your inheritance. Sing forth My praises forever and ever. Harken to My words of peace, security, and serenity. Yours is not a false hope but fashioned by My own hand, brought forth through adversity, but bringing strength, forbearance, and the ability to stand fast and see the salvation of your Lord. Faithful and true shall be the words you shall proclaim in the land of the living and I shall say of you, "Faithful and true, you did not faint but possessed your reward." Stand straight and tall, for My approval is with you and I shall not fail you. The beauty and majesty of fireworks, the endless display of My power. Get ready for a grand show. Waver not. Stand strong, immovable.

In the midst of confusion shall come a clear golden thread of light illuminating and making known My perfect will saying, "This is the way, walk ye in it." Fear not, wrestle not, but follow the steps one by one into My perfect and abiding will. Say not to your heart, "It is finished," but say to your heart, "It has just begun, and My God shall establish and bring forth all that He has proclaimed in the land of the living."

Steadily, steadily have you trudged the weary path, making sure along the way that I am before you. Steep has been the path in places and the food and water scarce. Now I say unto you, "Fear not, for the way is sure and the destiny secure." Be refreshed from the tedious time and come into an open place, flowing with My living water. (*Like an oasis; but Father, I don't even see the oasis, and it seems that the path is getting narrower and steeper. What do I do?*) Be calmed by this very thing; I am with you! My rod and My staff, they comfort you. I prepare a table before you in the presence of your enemies. Surely goodness and mercy shall follow you all the days of your life, and you shall dwell in the House of the Lord forever. You stand in the counsel of the Almighty. Fear not, but go forward unhindered by doubt. Walk firmly, confidently, and with great understanding, for I am with you and open the doors before you. I cause you to walk through them confidently, with faith and trust in My ability to cause you to prosper in the land of the living.

All is overcome by My Glory, My Presence within you. Sing and make known the Presence of your God. My Presence is within you, marking My territory within you. As you sing, you mark the territory for your God without. Shine forth My Light and declare to all, "My God reigns within and around me." It sets up a shield of dominion and proclaims to all the sovereignty of your King. Be a proclaimer of My sovereignty. It shall be to the delight of us both. Sing praises unto God, sing praises and the Glory of your God shall reign within your life to the Glory of God the Father.

For you have said unto Me, "The way is heavy and dark and the jungle is dense and dark," but I say unto you, "Fear not the darkness, for I am shining in the darkness to bring you through the darkness into My glorious light, never again to be overwhelmed by the darkness." You will understand those in the darkness and will have great compassion for them and it will melt your heart, and from your heart of compassion will come forth the healing they need to walk in My light with you. See, the darkness is giving way to the early morning light. With the darkness will go the heaviness and with My light will come My Glory and the freshness, lightness, laughter, and joy of My Spirit. You shall know the truth and the truth shall set you free, free to be who you are in Christ for the Glory of God. Say not to yourself, "I am alone," but say to yourself, "The God of the universe has chosen to love me with an everlasting love, and my heart shall rejoice in the land of the living, restored and made whole." Be set free and say unto Me, "The Glory of the Lord brings me to that place of freedom, well-being, and the Glory of the Lord is my inheritance and the lifter of My head."

Day 62

There are times and seasons. Winter is the time of seclusion and rest, reflection, healing, preparation, storms, and stretching and watching for the wave. Spring brings expanded vision, cleanup from the storms, renewed hope, and new vision—spotting the wave. Summer is implementation, riding the wave and the joy of fulfillment. Autumn is change and time to catch a new wave. Each season has its new challenges. Cling to Me in every thought, word and action. Rejoice in each season.

Tears are like dead leaves that fall from the tree in the fall. All appears bleak and finished as the beauty of the tree falls to the ground, leaving a stark reminder of what was and might have been. The dead leaves hang around all winter as a reminder of a day passed of great splendor, almost mocking the tree. But in the Spring—surprise—new life! Resurrection from the dead, more glorious than before, and the deadness of winter forgotten in the gloriousness of life renewed.

Your sights are too short. Look up and let Me reveal to you the eternal hope of the ages, the way of transformation. From saying, "I could, or I can," to saying, "The world was created by God to bring forth to the fullest and utmost all the promises from His heart to me in the most magnificent way possible." Now look up and see Me in everything. Did you not see Me in dead leaves? Now see Me in all that comes your way. Any word you say, any word you sing shall bear My Spirit. Even "dead leaves" carried a poignant message to your heart. Ask Me for a word over each and every event in your life that evokes strong emotion or causes concern and I shall answer from My heart to yours. For I would have you understand My ways and I would have you know the truth from My heart in each and every circumstance. So come to Me in high expectation that I shall teach you with love and precious communion. The door is open and the banquet is served in your honor. Now partake with joy, faithfulness, and excitement for what shall come forth as we commune together.

Your light has not blown out by the storm that blows and rails around you. Fear not that My light will go out, be snuffed out from you, for it will not! It is simply at times on pilot, awaiting the move from My hand to bring it into full flame. But even on pilot, it has the power to warm others and direct them My way. Fear not the seeming coldness of the fire. It is a time of healing and restoration, not a time of giving forth. Be at peace. Be not impatient. Let Me lay the groundwork with strength and correctness. Nothing shall be lost. It is all gain for My Kingdom.

Day 63

Haste makes waste. Fear not the weariness and slowed-down pace, for My Spirit works in the quiet of body, soul, and spirit. Hold fast and sense My Presence. Line upon line, precept upon precept shall continue to bring to you your appointed goal and dream. My heart sings for you and that song brings you to the accomplished goal. Stand still and know the salvation of your God. Enjoy the rest. Don't lock yourself into situations. My Spirit will prevail in you. My grace will bring you through, not your ability to cope. So be at peace, relax and let Me work wonders in your life and a capacity to love beyond measure. My Spirit is at work in you to bring forth much fruit. You have been stretched and pulled and have said "peace, peace," when there was no peace. Let Me work the peace within you. Let Me work the miracle of life within you. Let Me bring satisfaction within your bones. Fear of failure shall not drive you. Cease from your labors of stress. Let Me rise up in the midst of you and proclaim victory. Victory it shall be, full and complete, for My Spirit is alive within you.

A burst of springtime is coming your way, the clouds dispersed and the beauty and freshness and newness of Spring brought forth from a dark and dreary Winter of the soul. Burst forth into Spring and let Me be your closest companion of joy.

Stages, the victory comes in stages like climbing stairs. Be not fainthearted but march straight ahead undaunted by the passing scene. Mysteries unfold as you spend time with Me. Triumphant and glorious shall be the days ahead, filled with the Glory of My love. Restore the walls that have been broken down around people by My love and acceptance. For they shall see in you restoration by My hand of love, and it shall draw them toward the warmth, light, and truth of My love.

Sing for the night truly is over. Sing, for the new day truly has dawned. I shall go before you preparing the way and singing in your ear, "Come forth into the sunshine and play with Me, My child, and together we shall rejoice in the splendor of My creation." Wonders shall you see and truly you shall know the fresh, sustaining touch of your Creator and Friend.

In times past I have said to you, "Go forth, conquer the land and lay hold of the promises I have given thee." Today I say, "Struggle not with inconsistencies. Let Me do the choreography and pursue not easier ground, but flow with Me as I lead. You shall not miss out and I will not allow your foot to stumble. Straight are the pathways laid out by Me. Be at peace and watch the scenario unfold. So shall you see wonders beyond imagination and My Spirit shall rejoice over you and with you."

Line upon line, precept upon precept I have led you, opening unto you marvels and promises of My Kingdom. Laid out before you is My plan of the ages witnessed by those who would but see and in seeing they shall witness Me at work in you in a magnificent way. Be not afraid of My reluctance to go forward in areas of concern to you. Worry not that the day seems as night to your soul. Worry not that much of your life seems filled with questions and concerns, for My Word to you is yea and amen, and My love for you is constant and true. My plan for you goes forth unabated by times and seasons, for the times and seasons are all created by Me. So be at peace, knowing that I have created for you a panorama of blessing and purpose in your life to bring forth My will in all its fullness.

Day 64

Let go of the past! Walk into the future with great joy and freedom. My strength is with you for foreordained exploits. Strain not to see too far in the distance. Walk in peace with Me this day, fulfilling My call upon your life in small ways each day that build upon themselves to create all that I have proclaimed. Little bits each day create the finished creation. The doors shall open on time, and you shall go through each one at its appointed time. Confer with Me often in the times to come, for My wisdom shall come forth to confirm and establish you in all that you should do and pursue.

Call to Me and I will answer. My rod (protection) and My staff (guidance), they comfort thee. I have raised thee up as a standard bearer amongst My people to say, "Here is the way, walk ye in it." Straight and narrow is the path and it leads to life everlasting. Faithfulness and trustworthiness is the key to walking uprightly before Me. Stand tall in My Presence. See what I see and call forth what I call forth with singleness of mind and heart. Sing forth into the heavens and mighty shall the miracles be that come forth.

I have swept and made clean, and have established you on high ground, removed from the clamor and din of lower roads, filled with the muck and the mire of confusion. Stay on the high road that My Spirit creates within your heart, allowing you to rejoice in the completeness of My love and peace that brings forth My joy. Let Me fan the embers and provide for you labors that fulfill and spring forth capabilities of which you know not. Of My seasons, My times, and My ways, you are learning. Seek not to leave behind this season too quickly before it has brought forth the appointed fruit and wisdom. Settle in for the duration and fear not, for your faithfulness shall be known and rekindle faithfulness in others.

Life for you has been like dark silhouettes against the night sky, but I have held your hand and together we have walked through the darkness. I have held you steady and created within your heart a song and a melody to comfort and strengthen you along the way. It is not necessary for others to know the darkness of the night or the weight of the struggle, for I know and strengthen and sustain and cause your heart to sing in the night. Strange and fearsome has been the night, but you have seen the light of My smile upon you. My light has overcome the dark places in your life and overcome the dark night of your soul. The angels rejoice with you as you step forth each day in total reliance in Me and confidence in My steadfast love. I have held you in My arms and have stroked your hair, bringing comfort to your wearied soul. I have loved you with an everlasting love and now, together, we shall see the wearied one restored, the prisoner set free, and the lost found. Like hearts shall join with you who have counted the cost and marched forth to victory. You have counted the cost and fought the good fight and shouted the victory to a stagnant world. You shall comfort them as I have comforted you, and stroke their hair with love, and point them to Me, and I shall lift their burden and set them free. Glory in the highest!

Day 65

Each day is like a treasure handed to you on a silver platter, untouched by human hands, divine and holy. Treasure each day as a special gift, charted and laid out from the foundation of the earth. My blessed ones hear My voice and are satisfied. They know My heart of love toward them and walk unafraid. Stand strong and fearlessly in the confidence of My love and protection, for many are the opportunities to fall, but My hand sustains and protects you and causes you to flourish and grow. Stand guard against the enemy and shout for joy! Childlikeness and precision walk hand in hand by My Spirit. My Spirit proclaims victory over your life. Be refreshed this day.

You are as stained glass—beautiful pieces of glass, created by great pressure and heat, soldered and held together by My love and faithfulness. The Master craftsman works tirelessly and lovingly to create a masterpiece of beauty that shall last forever, a joy to the eyes and senses, enhanced by many beautiful and vibrant colors, proclaiming a statement of My perfection, faithfulness and love for My creation. Wrestle not with the creative process. Know that I shall complete what I have begun with perfection and you shall be delighted and rejoice as a favored child is overwhelmed with delight and gleeful joy because of gifts given by a doting Father. Know this, My child, the book of your life has been written, printed, and completed with nothing missing or overlooked. Rest in this knowledge. From your loving, doting Father.

Shiny bright like a new coin is My will for you—each morning and each day, prospering in every way. Steadfastness has been a virtue, transferred from My heart to yours. It has held you steady and secure when life was a blur. But now you shall see a better way, a way that shall make you rejoice and say, "To God be the Glory, great things He hath done." For now you shall see life can be fun, as you become one with My purpose and Son!

Day 66

Tides come and go. Seasons change. The magnitude of My Word to you changes as each year comes and goes. Silence has been golden throughout your life. Laughter has been a prize to be attained. Silver linings in the storms have abounded and you have seen and pondered them in your heart. My Word you have treasured. My song has been in your heart. My beauty has made your heart sing and My love has held you strong. It has been said, "There is music and laughter in your voice," but there shall be laughter and a new joy in your soul, My special gift to you. Come to the well and drink deeply, My child, that you might overflow and bubble merrily. Laughter it shall be, full and free. Tremendous things lie ahead, ready to be walked in and explored.

Snuggle in, My child, snuggle in. (*Saw myself on the Father's lap, holding on for dear life, and He snuggling me close, my head on His heart.*) It is a time for snuggling in and coming close. My heart has always been a resting, comforting place for you as your heart shall continue to be a resting place for others, in an increasing greater measure. Soak in My love. Fill up your tank. Filled to give, filled to give. Now you shall see the way it should be, careful to be ever filled with Me. Love them to Me. Love them to Me.

Ruminate not on the fragilities of man, but seek Me who is above all and the Creator of all. Circumstances shall not derail what I have created for you. Tattered and torn are many plans of those around you, but their Creator is the stable force in each of their lives, the Anchor upon which they can stand in faith unmoved. When the focus is on Me, one always lands on their feet from one of the enemy's bombs (land mines) along the path. Be fortified by My Word to your heart which is constantly available to you. Sing in the face of the enemy. Stand amazed at what I shall do with you, for you, and through you, for My Presence and Glory sustains you, leads, guides, and comforts you, and is the strong tower on which you stand and have your being.

Let Your Heart Sing

Behold, My servants shall sing for joy of heart
(Isaiah 65:14).

Day 67

I sing to you My song of deliverance. You shall hear it every day. Born through struggle to do it My way. Now very clearly you shall hear Me say, "Walk this way, walk that way, seek Me every day." Through every trial you have heard Me say, "Hold steady, for this is the way." Life shall no longer appear gray, for you have said, "Life was not meant to be this way, filled with sorrow and different shades of gray." My light shall shine about you to break forth from the darkness into the glorious light of noonday. So peace, be still. Let your heart sing. Let the joy of My Presence through your spirit ring. And let Me through that joy bring a refreshing that shall let your heart spring from sorrow to laughter which shall bring the answer to everything.

Change, great change—hard to keep up with, but you will. It will not be hard, but concerted effort will be required. Sing and maintain a high level of praise. Listen with your ear tuned to My voice. Seek My guidance as you respond and know that My Spirit is with you to guide and sustain you through the mine fields and the meadows. Time has been a blessing in your life. There will always be enough time to accomplish My perfect will. Trials have caused much pain and much growth. Stand tall, stand firm in your convictions, and you shall prevail.

I have poured you from glass to glass, straining out the impurities, creating pureness and wholeness, soundness and strength in your life. Answers shall come. It has been a test of time, trading in the familiar for the adventure. Hold on, for the ride shall bring forth an abundance of My Spirit. It shall no longer be a roller coaster ride, but as an eagle soaring through the sky with freedom and grace. Sing for the magnitude of My plan for you. Sing of My love and abundant grace in the lives of My children.

Seek Me daily and the frustration will leave. Draw from the deep well of My peace. Struggle not. My Spirit draws you daily to your destiny. Each grain of sand through the hourglass draws you closer, even when unobserved. Each day has its purpose, even when not evident to the eye or senses. My Spirit grows in strength in you each and every day. This is uppermost—trust My Spirit working through you. Timing, all is timing. Rejoice in My unfolding plan. The angels rejoice with you.

Be free! Be free from past experiences. Be free from past hopes and dreams. Be free to experience new realities of My giftedness to you and through you. Be free to see and dream anew!

Day 68

Hasten not to race or flee. Just be at peace with Me. Much growth has and shall continue to be manifested in this place of contentment, warmth, love, laughter, and joy. Obstacles have been overcome, and now comes forth a new thing in your life, complete in every way. You shall know what it means to play, and yet know My way every day for your life. Life and sincerity shall flow from your heart with a strength you have not known. Strength, and the ability to communicate with strength of will and love. Stand strong, My child, in the power of My love. The issues of life are settled within your heart and you are ready to move on with great strength and ability, directed by My love.

It truly is a time of refreshment, for you have been through the storm and I have kept you from harm. And after the storm there is calmness, fragrance, beauty, newness, and a rainbow proclaiming the truth of My promises. The fulfillment is sure, so keep your life pure, and the joy and freedom that is coming forth shall restore your soul.

I love you, My child. Know this and rejoice. All else is secondary. Rejoice, and be glad, for My Spirit hovers about you, is in you and enlivens you. The past is past! The present is now and is My gift to you. Savor each morsel of My present and Presence. Be captivated by its gloriousness. Be enraptured by the preciousness of the present. The future will hold its own gloriousness, but the Present holds all you need to be catapulted into the future. Be estranged from the past, captivated by the present, and confidently secure about the future. It is all yours, but *now* is My precious gift to you to be enjoyed and treasured. My Spirit continues to encourage and make known the precious present. Be enlightened, encouraged, and enhanced.

Revel in the completeness of all I have created for you to experience, that you might proclaim My faithfulness to a dying world. Have you not tasted of the death that is the everyday portion of the world, and have I not said, "The just shall live by faith and rejoice in the God of their Fathers through Jesus Christ their Lord"? Continue to declare My faithfulness to you and draw upon that faithfulness day by day, for I am with you and nothing shall derail you, but you shall declare that all has been to the Glory of your God. Faithfulness is the key, My faithfulness to you and your faithfulness to Me. Rejoice in the quiet days of reflection. Rejoice in the hectic days of service, and rejoice in the days of shared love. They all are by My hand, none better than the other.

Stillness and quietness of soul brings great gain. It is where you began your adventure with Me and how I taught you to stand, fearlessly and triumphantly. Together, we shall continue to stand and rejoice in the outcome. Come apart unto Me often to refresh your heart.

Songs, songs, songs, and more songs ringing in your heart and soul in the night and in the day, ringing in your heart to say, "I love you." I am here to stay! I will not go away, but shall cause your heart to sing with revelation knowledge. It will cause others' hearts to sing and be satisfied with My goodness to them. Stories I shall tell them in the midst of the song, causing their hearts to long to know Me more. I shall pour from your heart to theirs strong evidences of My love for them. And they shall see, through you, that they, too, can be conduits of My Presence and love.

Day 69

Straightforward words of love you shall hear from My Spirit to yours, calling you forth from the shadows into My marvelous light. The shadows will no longer be able to contain you but will thrust you out where My Glory can be seen. Glorious are the days ahead. Eye hath not seen nor ear heard the marvelous blessings ready to be bestowed upon My children. The sifting has been relentless and steady. It has been long and tedious but well worth the struggle.

My Spirit races on before you, opening the doors, causing hearts to respond with favor, with perfect timing, causing your heart to soar. My Spirit abounds with blessings. When the timing is perfect, I pour out abundant blessings autographed to you (signed by the Father's own hand). Now is the time for My abundant grace to fall upon you in this special place of renewal, restoration, and reformation. Your life and face shall reflect My Glory and My grace as you step by step fulfill My destiny for you. Be established in this place. It has been a place of sorrow and pain, but now it shall be a place of great gain, as together we proceed each day, confident in every way. I shall do all to My Glory through you as I have promised to do. Be at peace and rejoice as each piece of the puzzle comes together in completeness and beauty.

Your life is like a song. The melody weaves in and out and comes together, forming perfect harmony with grace. Each note and word fits perfectly, forming a beautiful whole. Many never get past the halting, labored opening verse to get to the fluid chorus. It is the chorus of a song that gives the most freedom and joy to the singer and to the listener alike.

Straight paths of My making stretch out before you, unhindered and untouched by human hands. Straight narrow paths of My choosing. I have strengthened you. I have created within you the dynamic needed to constrain those languishing on the sidelines of My will. They will see and know My power within you that has been tapped and made available to them to bring forth My will in their lives. They will never be the same again. They may believe they have escaped unscathed from My Presence in you, but they will not. They shall be drawn even after you are gone by an invisible gossamer thread that was created by their contact with you. It is a thread that draws them to Me. Have you not seen in the past the power of that gossamer thread? Take great joy in the smallest of contacts for My Kingdom, for much is accomplished in the smallest of contacts. Judge not the power of those contacts. Simply move on with confidence and joy, for My Spirit is at work, drawing in every instance. Those who know Me not move in serpentine trails. But as I draw them ever closer, their trails straighten out to portray My stability and steadiness in their lives, hence, the straight paths of My righteousness.

Plant your feet solidly in the security of My love and confidence in My faithfulness. Prizes go to the strong and secure in Me. You have stood strong. Reflect on the many times you have stood through the storm as winds blew with trees toppling all around you, but you stood. Time has stood still in your heart as the world has swirled around you. Time shall take on new dimensions of meaning and fullness. Be encouraged as you see Me move on your behalf and bring into the present the promises of the past that were always for the future. Be encouraged as you stand in that place of fulfillment brought forth by My grace and love. My faithfulness has made it so.

Day 70

Strange happenings have caused you to ponder and wonder what you had done to cause them. Wonder not but know that each happening has caused you to grow and reflect on My goodness to you. (*Father, what do you see for me this year?*) I see My songbird flying full and free! I hear you singing the mighty song of the free and redeemed. I see you rising to every occasion with a song in your heart and praise on your lips. And finally, I see a passion in your life that brings life to many! See and rejoice! Hear and revel in the hearing! The strong shall become stronger and the blessed shall bless!

As you continue to know My gifts and blessings to you, the skies will become bluer and the flowers brighter, and you will never be bored or lonely for I am always there opening new doors of delight to your heart. Strength, strength of character, fortitude, resilience, and the knowledge of My love and heart—all gifts I have bestowed upon you in abundance. Strength of will, that will to do My will in the face of all obstacles and temptations. Fortitude to stand in the midst of the storm and the resilience to rejoice and sing praise to Me in the midst of the storm. The knowledge of My heart shall increase and you shall know beyond the shadow of any doubt the abundance of My love. Stand in amazement at what I shall do. Be released this day from the fear of rejection and isolation. It shall not be! This now is a reality in your heart!

Your Father, who has created you for this day and for this moment, has spoken forth the creative word, "Come forth!" Be all I have created you to be. Do all I have created you to do. See all I have created you to see. My Spirit calls you forth this day! Bright are the days ahead, filled with adventure and light. Mighty are the days ahead that have been born out of the struggle to stand. Standing has been My plan for you through the years. It has been the formation of what you see and know. Standing is never easy. It is wearisome, but the rewards are great. Be encouraged this day as you continue to stand in My Presence with faith, hope, and love.

Traumatic weeks, months, and years have made you transparent, sincere, and trusting in Me. The weeks and the years have passed forming within you a trilogy of faith, hope, and love. But the greatest of these is love, love of My people, love of the truth, and love of the Trinity—Father, Son, and Holy Spirit. Within your heart beats the rhythm of My heart, a steady beat that only grace can give. You have depended on My grace to carry you through and thus extend that grace to others, knowing that grace can turn failure into success, death into life, and sorrow into joy. My grace has been sufficient for you and shall continue to uphold you and make a way for you. See, I have made a way for you through the midst of the storm, through the desert place, and through every trial and tribulation that has come your way. Amidst all you have seen and heard has been My abiding peace and love. My hand covers and protects you and gives you life and stability. Be at peace and rejoice with contentment and confidence in the outcome. You shall declare the Glory of God in thought, word, and deed. Continue to prepare as My hand of deliverance works in your life.

Seek Me every day that you might be sustained and strong in every way. Fashioned precisely according to every detail is My will and plan for you. You have rejoiced in the making. Now you shall rejoice in the fulfillment of the dream. It comes forth speedily as the light over the mountains of the new day, resplendent in every way.

Day 71

Through the years My Spirit has lifted you up, and shown you a marvelous way of contentment and peace through the length of your days. I have blessed you in all of your ways. Through the years My Spirit has comforted you and lifted you out of the mire. Now your feet shall dance and your heart rejoice. You have come through the midst of the fire. So rejoice and sing, let your praises ring for My Spirit has caused you to see that no matter what the circumstance, My love for you will always be the source of your strength, full and free. Do you believe this? (*Yes, Father.*) Never doubt the power of My love and direction in your life. It will never become less. It will only become more. You did not falter. You remained true to your convictions. I have sustained you. I have led you. I have tested you, but you have remained faithful to the end. You stood firm, you stood strong. You were faithful to your calling. Life, I speak life to your heart! You have not begun to know the power of My love within you.

Stranger than fiction is the stream of your life, fashioned by your Father's hand to bring forth My handiwork in due time. Breakneck speed is not My way. Be at peace, My child, as I fashion your life in My image, complete in every way. The ravages of time shall not harm you, but shall enhance you. So fear not the passing of time. Time is your friend as it works within you treasures to be enjoyed and beheld. You are My treasure, transformed and changed into My image. Rejoice and be glad in My Spirit of truth coming forth in your life. Fear not, each moment of each day is protected by My hand.

My child, (*Yes, Lord*) skip lightly, joyfully, gracefully, but resolutely, for strong and secure shall you be with every step you take and every decision you make as we go forward and as the future becomes the present and My promises to you become the fulfillment of your dreams and wishes. Sure, secure, and sound shall every step be orchestrated and directed by My heart of love toward you. Your heart shall sing and your praises ring in exhilaration and joy, pure joy.

Day 72

Stability and contentment go together to bring you to a place of fulfillment and confidence. In contentment and peace shall my promises come forth. Bridge the gap from hoping to knowing through joy, thanksgiving, and trust. Trials have come and gone but each one has left a deposit of strength, resourcefulness, and faithfulness within you. You have gone the extra mile with a smile and words of encouragement to many. They have seen the struggle to survive and yet they have seen My Glory about you. The struggle has been great, but the rewards shall be greater. Secure in My love you have been, able to see Me in every occurrence, willing to lay down your life if need be, knowing I have laid down My life for you. The struggles have weighed you down and caused you to pull in the corners of your tent pegs, but now I say, "Open up the tent. Let the sun stream in, and I shall expand the tent pegs of your life to magnify My Name."

Feast your eyes on the prizes coming your way. Some are the desires of your heart resurrected. Some are the fulfillment of dreams past. Some seemed to be the figment of your imagination and some the cry of your heart. You shall sit in amazement as you see the multitude of blessings coming your way. See the mystery of times past come into focus. See the answers to questions asked revealed. Expectations shall be high as you walk through this appointed time. Fluctuations, renovations, and revelations shall be the order of the day as you draw ever closer to the fulfillment of My words spoken.

My strength has prevailed in your life to make you strong and resilient. Measure not physical strength with strength of character and strength of resolve. The heavens declare the victory of one who has walked the weary miles and prevailed. With a song in your heart and in your mouth, you shall continue to march forth with flags of victory flowing in the wind as you walk, for it shall be a walk of victory, not one of struggling to remain upright and prevailing. Sincerity of heart has kept you straight on target. Now the shout of victory shall lead you forth and cause your heart to burst forth with song and rejoice. Battalions shall go forth in waves and you shall be amongst them, waving your flag of jubilation and victory!

Now It Begins

*But you shall receive power
when the Holy Spirit has come upon you;
and you shall be witnesses to Me in Jerusalem,
and in all Judea and Samaria,
and to the end of the earth*
(Acts 1:8).

Day 73

Seasons of change are here to stay. Released are the doors of blessing that bring forth those changes. Finances shall grow and expand, and the ability to receive and know My voice shall expand and grow. The letter of the law shall never refer to you, for you shall go forth with My Spirit of praise and thanksgiving radiating from your face and spilling forth from your mouth—reserved for thee from eternity, your destiny, and your place. Truth, stranger than fiction, shall continue to show you the way. Now it begins!

Upon the waters of life shines forth the Glory of God. Your countenance shall shine forth the Glory of God as never before, for you have gone through the valleys and maintained a steady stride, unbroken by the weights and brokenheartedness of the way. So lay down the past, give it all to Me. Lay down the past and you will see that it all has brought you to this place of fulfillment and grace. Lighthearted joy shall replace the heaviness of the past and cause you to see Me as never before. Rejoice in the now! You have stood in storm after storm and I have kept you from harm. So step forth this day, free in every way to express this deep love in your heart for Me; the windows of Heaven shall overflow and shower you with gifts untold, more than you can hold. They shall cause you to be bold. The story will be told and retold.

Ministry is a covenant with Me. You receive from Me and then give it out. Receive and give, receive and give. So life is a covenant. Receive life from Me and give it to others. Receive and give. Receive life, give life. Receive life, give life through your words, through your prayers and through your actions. Life is tangible. You can see life and you can transfer life. Only I can create life. Only I can give life. You must receive life from Me and then you can pass it on. Receive and pass on. Receive and pass on. But receiving life is a commitment, and thus the covenant.

Facilitate and create! My gift to you! Your gift to others. Your strength shall return by leaps and bounds that you might give My strength and hope to others. Sing in the night! Sing in the day! Sing always, for My light shines forth through your songs of praise. Stand strong in the knowledge of My love and compassion over you, for you shall continue to share that love and compassion with all you meet and come into contact with. They shall feel the warmth of My Spirit upon them as they come near you. It will open their ears to hear and recognize My heart toward them. So sing, My child. My Spirit shall rule through your songs of praise. I have made a way through the wilderness and now you see the oasis of My choosing, an oasis of joy, refreshment, and direction for you and the same for all who come near you. Your journeys shall take you far and wide, but My oasis of love, peace, beauty, and joy shall continue with you forever.

Day 74

You have struggled long and hard to come into this place. You still feel inadequate to the task, but all that you need is within you to complete and fulfill the tasks at hand. Your destiny is sure and secure. Struggle not to fulfill that destiny but start each day with Me securely in the place of authority and love over your life. Take each day as it comes, rejoicing in Me and free to move, love, and be refreshed in Me. The enemy would love to make you feel pressured and inadequate. Refuse to be moved by him. When anxiety arises, "Come away My beloved." Let Me calm your inner being, moment by moment. Remember, running in place does not accomplish the goal, but a calm and unrushed step-by-step progression toward the goal. Be not pressured. Each day will have within it that step or steps moving forward with confidence and peace.

Divine strategies have come into play. Strong leadings shall continue to come your way. Influences shall guide you each day as My Spirit moves upon you. Be that standard bearer of truth. A tightrope is not My way. Be open and let the chips fall where they may. Be established in My love. That is trust and forbearance—trust in My ability to work all for your good and forbearance to know I will protect you as you give out grace to others. You are to be a standard bearer of forbearance and grace. It is by My hand and you shall stand and show forth My love and acceptance, total acceptance in humility and truth.

Be as the eagle in flight and see as from above, looking down with eagle eyes. Fly above the smog and pollution. Be set free from religiosity. Fly high in the sky. Rely on My ability to bring the air currents for you to catch. Be released and set free. Let your world be from sea to sea, not from tree to tree. Open your eyes that you might see the mighty catch I have for thee. Be not astounded at what I shall bring as you take wing.

Just sing your song all the day long, through the late night hours into the new dawn. The bird truly sings for the pure joy of singing praise to its Maker and friend. The world beats a path to the door of one who has found peace within. (*Lord, I don't feel like I have peace within.*) Then sing with abandon. My peace will return and turn the rain into sunshine. Be lifted up into the higher realms of praise. Be set free from the pull downward. Fly high in the heavenlies where the songs of angels are heard and one can see the panoramic view. Fly high in the sky. Fly above the problems and remain unruffled in My mantle of peace.

A sounding board to many you shall be, causing them to readily see the pits and captivities they have fallen snare to in times past, causing the pain to last and last. And now because you have broken through, they too shall begin to muse and see the trap they've fallen through, and one by one they'll break the trap and see My blessings fall in their laps. Together you'll see the enemy flee and put to flight all evidence of the fight. My Spirit shall bloom where the enemy took flight, proclaiming victory to all in sight.

Day 75

Seasons of change have woven the tapestry of your life—here a valley, there a mountain high. But in each place the touch of the Master's hand that makes the valleys the same as the mountains, touched and sustained by love, each moment a gift of grace. The style has changed, but the message remains the same, "See My face of love and grace reflected in this place. Struggles cease with full release, for the Spirit knows you cannot fail along this trail. My love has made it so."

A songbird chirps and sings, welcoming the new day. It proclaims and calls forth the new day with joy, exuberance, and faith that it will be a great day, filled with the love and blessings of a benevolent and loving God and Father. So are you to chirp and sing, proclaiming My loving works to a sleepy world. Continue to chirp and sing, calling forth the blessings of the new day. Birds are unafraid and confident in their freedom, for they fly high in the sky where predators do not go. Sound forth My love and faithfulness. Sound forth My ability to heal and save. Go forth in My Name proclaiming to all, there is a place of quiet rest, safe in the arms of God!

Straight words of love I speak. (*Lord, they speak straight to my heart.*) You have listened and blossomed and bloomed. The beauty is real and the fragrance is sweet. The path you have trod has been no small feat. Now with words of love straight from your heart, you shall impart insight gained only from traveling the road of the trusting heart, listening intently, My words to impart. See Me reach out to hearts poised to receive. See Me restore hearts that mourn and grieve. Among My treasures I'll be found, and their hearts will leap at the gentle sound of My voice resounding clear as they hear, "I love you," with clarity and grace. Hear Me comfort, exhort, and impart just the right things that will warm their hearts. You will see, hear, know, and sense My Presence as My seed you sow.

Out of sight, out of mind is the way of the world, but not the way of My Kingdom on earth. My Spirit goes out to heal at any moment of any day from My faithful ones who hear the call to love and pray, opening the way for My Spirit to move. You are a candle lighter. I use you to spark hope, light, joy, and enlightenment into the lives of others. It only takes a spark to get a fire going. You are a fire starter in My people. Bask in My Glory. It gets the fire burning hotter in your soul, attracting others to partake with exuberance and joy.

It's called honor! Honor My wishes! Honor those around you and honor thyself! Seek to walk in honor in all that you do and say. Dishonor destroys. Honor brings life and wholeness. Stand up to dishonor. Refuse it at every turn. You will recognize it more and more. Discernment is recognizing dishonor. You will learn more and more as each day goes by. Trials come from dishonor. No longer will dishonor sneak up on you and entrap you. You shall recognize it for what it is, lack of love! Lack of love for their God, for you, and for themselves. Carry on now with confident trust that you will recognize dishonor at every turn and deal with it with My love.

Day 76

Fiery darts from the enemy have sought to derail you and throw you off track. But a humble heart stays on track. Respect and love go hand in hand, the foundation of My plan. Steer clear of strife and division. Take your stand to remain on neutral ground, forbearing and releasing blessing. It's a mystery to be told. A truth that cannot be bought or sold. In My Presence one can simply be unafraid of human frailties. Seek My heart and you will see confusion leave. Strength of purpose standing strong, rejoicing in My Presence all the day long. Seek the giver of all things. Seek the peace My Presence brings.

Can you see Me in yourself? That is the goal. A picture is worth a thousand words. Be a picture of My faithfulness and love. Strategic points along the way point you in the right direction. The strategy has always been, that I would be seen through you. Let Me paint the picture clearly in your life. Straight as an arrow shall the message be for all to see, a picture of Me seen through you.

My agenda is set in place and is being laid out and achieved. Worry not as to the execution of it. It truly is in My hand and you shall reap the benefits and rewards. Hurry not to see and understand. Be at peace and take each day as it comes, as it arrives. Strive not to fulfill. Go your way rejoicing.

Strength, I have promised strength to your body, soul, and spirit. Step up higher in the knowledge of My love. Step up higher in the abundance of My Spirit of grace. You have longed to see My face. It is reflected in My grace. Be reflected in My grace. It is a place reserved for you. In the midst of the clamor and din is My peace, a place reserved to walk in. And together we'll find a steady peace of mind that transcends every hindrance conceived. It is yours because you have believed. There is a place where My Spirit of grace breaks down all barriers to the soul. It is found with a price, not a life that seems nice, but one fought on the battlefield for gain, the battle for freedom and life. It's a battle that must be fought, for it is there that is wrought victories of spirit, body, and soul—the goal, that you might be whole.

The enemy would hand you over on a silver platter if possible. But My Word to you is, from the foundation of the world I have known you. I have loved you, protected you, and adorned you with My precious gifts. It is My good pleasure to fulfill your destiny and to prepare you for things to come. Say unto your heart, "My God is the terminator of all that comes against me. My God stands in judgment against all who lift their hands against me, and My God is the lifter of my head." Now be on guard against the enemy's attempt to stomp in your yard. Grab hold of My hand by faith. Don't take the bait (fear). My Spirit shall refresh and restore. See, I have opened many doors for you. And together we shall go through them one by one and destroy the works of the enemy that he has done. See Me first in everything you do. Let My Spirit come shining through. And you will know without a doubt that My Spirit will bring it about.

Go Forth With Praise and Thanksgiving

You have turned for me my mourning into dancing;
You have put off my sackcloth
and clothed me with gladness,
To the end that my glory may sing praise
to You and not be silent.
O Lord my God, I will give thanks to You forever
(Psalm 30:11-12).

Day 77

Eliminate waste (hurt, fear, and all negatives). Replace it with love and faithfulness. Counteract the negative by the positive. Speak life. Be a proclaimer of My peace. Establish My love. Surrounded by My angels, you shall go forth unafraid. You have been established in My peace. You have been established in My love. You have let go of the overwhelming forces of fear and rejection and have looked to Me for your worth and abundance. I shall carry you forth with ease and simplicity and it shall be known to My Glory that all is well with your soul, for I have established it. Go forth with praise and thanksgiving and establish a trail for others to walk upon proclaiming My goodness and love. My love overshadows you and protects you and carries you forth into uncharted territory. Go forth without fear. Simply go forth in the security of My love. Strong, immovable, and filled with My power are those who stand in My grace and proclaim the divine providence and sustaining power of their God.

The world says, "Three strikes and you are out." I say unto you, Whither thou goest, I will go with you. From the crown of your head to the soles of your feet shall My Spirit be with you, abide with you, and rest upon you. Enter into each day with expectancy and the ability to see Me in every event.

Faithfulness is a virtue obtained as one stands faithful in the face of unfaithfulness. Love is a virtue obtained as one stands loving in the face of unlovingness. One becomes sweet in the face of anger. One becomes content when one stands strong in the presence of discontent. (*But Lord, wisdom has to be simply a gift from You because one asks and stays in Your Presence.*) Destiny fulfilled is the greatest joy, for it brings together faithfulness, love, contentedness, and wisdom—all the gifts of My Spirit brought together by living in My Presence.

Fortify your stand of faith. (*How do I do that, Lord?*) As you are doing, spending time in My Presence. Come forth in such a way that those who know shall say, "Among His treasures she was found and her heart rejoiced at the gentle sound of My voice, for to hear My voice was her choice." And together as we share from sea to sea the blessing that hearing My voice can bring, your heart shall sing and bring forth treasures never before heard or seen. The pathway lies ahead of you and together we shall walk, sing, and enjoy the blessings each day brings. For within each day My treasures are found. Not one day shall fall to the ground, but shall be blessed with My very best. So forward now, My little one, unafraid and knowing full well that I your God, your faithful Friend, know the beginning from the end.

Day 78

Struggles come when you doubt My ability to carry you through to completion. (When we feel like we're losing ground and it depends on us to be good enough.) Rest in My ability to accomplish it through you. Put to flight all worries and struggles to maintain the status quo. We shall overcome the status quo and go forth to greater victories.

Truth sets the captives free that they might be all they were created to be. The sky is the limit when truth is walked in and believed. Truth burns away the clouds so that the Sonshine might shine through the dimness and proclaim victory. Struggles abound outside of victory's light. It actually seems like night in the light of day when the enemy has his way. But the way of truth received always causes the heart to believe and then comes forth the victory shout as the enemy we route.

Struggle not! Restrain yourself from apparent stress. My Word to you is freedom in the midst of hardship and pain. Rise above the shadows. Come into My marvelous light, above the clouds and shadows. Be restored in My abundance of joy and freedom of heart. Be not bogged down with the transitory. See Me in each moment of every day. Carry not the burden of the immediate. Be not driven by the immediate. Stand strong in My Presence. Be not dismayed but abound in the joy of being. I am with you!

Sustained to bless and be a blessing. Set into place are the foundation stones. Now the walls can go up quickly. (*Father, what are the foundation stones?*) Truth, faithfulness, and love.

Streamlined. I will make you streamlined once again. But this time, it will not be for acceptance and love. It will be orchestrated from above. For the treasures I have for you in store, will be the opening of the door to bring forth the prophecy foretold, the worth of it like solid gold. Chart a course. Light the fire. Maintain your heart's desire by constant looking just to Me. You'll see those extra pounds flee. For built within the Master Plan is a body that moves with flexibility. Sunrise to sunset, let it be your goal to eat the foods that nourish body and soul. But in the gathering of the night, let those foods be put to flight. And in their stead, a cup of tea with Me will sustain thee. Let it be your solid goal, the strengthening of body, spirit, and soul. For the days ahead are filled with grace, but it will help you be prepared to walk in this place.

Time and time again I have uprooted you and placed you on a new trail and you have rejoiced at the newness and awesomeness of My plan. Now I do a new thing in your life that shall outshine all the other paths that you have taken. You shall see such beauty on this new path and you shall rejoice at the ability of your heart to take it all in and respond with joy. Bask in the warmth of My smile and know as never before My ability to create and recreate. Seasons of change have formed your existence in Me. Change has brought forth the formation of the fruit and trust has caused it to ripen. Now the fruit shall bring forth the change and gladden your heart.

Restoration of what has been lost has come at a great cost. But the fulfillment foretold has made you bold. See the future through My eyes of love. Blessing is cumulative. Watch it unfold. I'll give you more blessing than your heart could hold. But now the Master Plan set forth. Nothing shall close the open doors. Kick up your heels. Laugh with Me. The time has come. You are set free!

Day 79

There is a mystery unfolding. Keep your ear to the ground. Each piece of the puzzle shall be found. A piece here and a piece there. Some seem to come from thin air. But in your heart you shall know. This one comes from above, not below. Seek the Giver, not the gift, even though the gift gives such a lift. Lift up your heart to Me. With the passing of each day you shall see bits and pieces beyond the veil. Each bit and piece leaves a discernable trail. It's not a matter of chance. So lay your burdens at My feet. I know the details that need to be complete. Piece by piece, the puzzle will become clear: a picture painted by My own hand.

Lasting results you'll see, brought about by your resolve to just be. The hustle bustle surrounding you still will fade into the background, replaced by a will to be at peace in My Presence. You've found the secret: don't be run into the ground. My Spirit resides in a heart that can rest even in trials and struggles. My peace is best. Attained by commitment, My direction to know, by listening, obeying, My peace you shall sow into the lives of those whose hearts long to know, the secret of just letting go. Let Me handle the cares of this life, all that wears upon the heart and the strife. Be a restorer of peace. It will bring sweet release.

I will bring many your way. Their hearts will reach out to you, for they will find within your heart a resting place, a place of refuge. Seek not to be the restorer of their souls, but seek to be that peaceful resting place for their souls. For as they rest and take stock of from whence they came, they shall see and be healed. Hasten not to break the bondages, but first let them rest in your heart and then I can take away the parts that bind, constrict, and bring pain. It shall be great gain.

A light unto your path have I been in times past, a beacon light to establish and make your way clear. Up till now, you have proceeded with caution, but with confidence in My guiding hand. The way has been made clear in many ways unknown to you as you have gone forth in faith and confidence in My ability to sustain you and accomplish in your life the mighty goal. Now I do a new thing, brought forth to please you and set you apart for new avenues of service and accomplishment. Times of unsettling have been the order of the day for many years. Now I will settle and establish you in new arenas of service and functioning in My Kingdom. The past has faded away through times of stress and apparent trouble. I have spoken many times that now I do a new thing in your life brought forth by My hand of love. Established you shall be, confident in the groundwork that has been laid throughout the years in your life. I have spoken, and it has come forth. I have proclaimed, and the doors have opened and brought you forth into new vistas of service. Now, I say, Rise up! Come forth! Be established in this place that I might send you forth to proclaim My loving-kindness to a lost and dying world, enslaved by an ignorance of My love. An ambassador of My love you shall be, and the doors shall open wide that you might proclaim My love with abandon!

Secret places of My abiding Presence you shall find as you persistently come into My Presence with love and devotion. I have carried you in My arms of love. I have kept you secluded away in the protective place of My love. The heavens proclaim the Glory of God. You shall proclaim along with the heavens the Glory and protective love of your Father and God. Sweet communion shall be the order of the day and your heart will be bursting to say, "My Lord and my God have shown me the way to life and liberty."

Day 80

As you are transparent, what will show through will be strength, confidence, and security, brought about by the absolute faith in My love and protection. Be not afraid to be vulnerable—vulnerable with strength and confidence in Me. You don't stand alone. If you could see the prayers that go up for you each and every day, your heart would sing and rejoice for the love My Spirit brings.

Be bold, be strong, be confident. Shine forth My light. Be brave. For I am confident in you. I have made you bold. I have made you strong. I have made you brave. I have made you confident to do My will. The bottom line—you are in My care. In that place is confident trust. My Presence will become more precious to you as you continue to step out in faith. I will stretch you and you will grow in grace, truth, and freedom. Freedom to think and know My will and My good pleasure in your life. The walls of self-imposed restrictions shall continue to come down with a thud and in their place will be the fragrance and beauty of My heart and My Spirit in your every action and thought. Measure each day by the Glory of My Presence.

The sky's the limit, you will impart My love, into the niches and crevices of each aching heart. Be diligent, be faithful, My glory you'll see as you minister My love to every need. And then, what a treasure, each one shall come forth. Bursting into fulfillment, their spirits shall soar, and proclaim My goodness to all they shall see. My precious provision to all who believe.

Time Is Your Friend

*And we know that all things
work together for good
to those who love God*
(Romans 8:28).

Day 81

Passages of time clear the way for new beginnings and new openings in the Spirit. Time is your friend and brings forth the blessings spoken of. So many passages of time in the growth of a tree before it ever sets fruit. Even when it flowers, the flowers fade and fall off, making way for the fruit. So it has been in your life. Lasting fruit takes time. Fear not because of time. It is your friend. Milestones along the way refresh and bring to mind the promises. Resist not the parameters of time. I say again, "It is your friend."

Recapture the fragrance of fun. Be the Pied Piper who sings and dances along the trail of blessing, leading others in the joy and fragrance of My love, freedom, laughter, and joy. No good thing do I withhold from My loving, joyful, trusting children.

Steadfast and immovable you have been, able to stand up to the toughest trial. Now I do a new thing in your life—a turnaround to brighten your days. And days shall turn into years and the Spirit of the Living God would say unto you, "The end shall be as the beginning, filled with My Presence and love." Masterfully I weave the thread and create the very details of your life to bring forth My creation of exquisite detail. Surely My hand is not short to create and fashion a masterpiece to delight My heart. Rejoice in the making.

My child, My heart croons over you a song of love. The melody sweet, with the fragrance from above. Can you not hear it within your ear, eliminating all stress and fear? Listen to its peaceful sound. Within its melody, My love is found. I sing to you, My child, that you might sit with Me awhile. And listen to its silent call, proclaiming My peace to one and all. So listen with an ear to hear, My songs of love to you so clear.

The fulfillment of your heart and dreams comes hidden and unseen. And then in the fullness of day, suddenly eyes see what was there all along but hidden from view. Hope fulfilled is the hope of all who dream. The wise man seeks My plan, then stands unmoved by the passing scene. (*Father, many have stood unmoved by the passing scene only to see the plan changed and re-arranged. But nothing can take away the growth that standing proclaims.*) The human heart was created to beat with the strength of My love. It seeks to know the strength of My love. And in the fulfillment of that knowledge found, it continually seeks for higher ground. Be alert as you climb that mountain high, as you are tempted to groan and sigh, that every crest and level taken, requires trust and faith that you not feel forsaken. For as you climb that mountain high, that seems to reach clear to the sky, new levels of understanding must parallel each level unending. So listen closely, My precious child. Be alert, don't let the enemy bite and rile. But with each passing day, lift up your heart and say, "This too was God's special day."

Day 82

Sincere praise lifts up the heart into realms of Glory, My Presence, and proclaims My goodness. Shallow praise rings hollow in the heart and the ears and proclaims emptiness and futility. Lasting gifts of My Spirit come forth through sincere praise and thanksgiving, brought forth from a trusting, loving heart. Seek to walk with steadfast abandon to My heart and will. Shallow ways bring forth shallow deeds. My ways of faithfulness and love bring forth My will upon the earth.

Sift through and you will continue to find the gold nuggets of lasting value to enhance and open the way for My Spirit to be glorified in you and in those around you. Be not astounded at the mighty and awesome things to come. Each day is another piece of the massive tapestry being formed of lasting value and worth. It has seemed slow, laborious, and greatly lacking in detail, but know that within My framework of time, much has been accomplished and much shall stand the passage of time. Here a little, there a little; each day compiling a masterpiece of great beauty to draw the nations of the world to the warmth and safety of My love. Continue your quest for the gold. It is a quest worthy of My love and the fulfillment of My Word. It seems to be a marathon that you are running for the gold; but know this, the quest is worthy of the effort to run the race. You are surrounded by My love and protection as you run. Release unto Me all anxiety, for I am with you.

Forgiveness is the key to cause the enemy to flee. Stolen ground is his to grab. He'll always take a stab. Release his hold by being bold to stand in forgiveness and say, "I refuse to be offended this day."

Steal away that your time with Me be as treasure restored. Let not the enemy require of thee time set aside for great gain and joy with Me. Can you not see that time has been robbed from you and in its place you have reaped frustration and toil. I shall restore unto you the joy of your salvation. I have said, "The sky is the limit." Our relationship has no bounds but those bounds released, portrayed, and accepted from the enemy of your soul. Stray not from the center of My will for thee. My will for thee is to do the will of My Father, which is intimacy with God. Come into the Bridal Chamber. It is there where I can bestow upon you My love, peace, freedom, and purest joy. It is there where impartation is released and those attributes longed for are bestowed upon My beloved. Situations fade into the background and answers are obtained. Can you not see it, this place of favor and release from bondage? Never leave this place. Be always in the arms of your Beloved. Many times you have heard, "Singleness of heart and mind is the pathway to intimacy sustained with your Beloved." Stolen moments will cease to be the way. Now comes forth a life that sings, hidden away in the Bridal Chamber of the King.

It is a fine line between faith and presumption. Faith calls forth those things that have been proclaimed by the Spirit of God. Presumption calls forth that which has been proclaimed by the heart of man. Be the friend of faith and the foe of presumption. Herald the way of My Spirit as proclaimed by My prophets. (*Father, how do I know the difference?*) The heart knows. Listen to your heart and respond appropriately. Steer clear of those who proclaim My ways without My heart. It is a mixed word incapable of being leaned on with all your weight. The Spirit of the Lord proclaims truth through love. If love is lacking, so is truth. You cannot have one without the other. First comes love, then comes truth. Reversed, truth is not revealed, but a heart that needs love. Be sure of this very thing, that one cannot mock love without mocking truth. They go hand in hand.

Day 83

Religion versus lavish worship. Religion is man bypassing God. Worship is man coming to God in intimacy. Avoidance verses intimacy. Religion, the letter of the law, brings death. Worship by the Spirit brings life. Religion is the form. Worship is the substance. Worship brings My Glory, My Presence, and My goodness. Religion brings deadness, separation, and My wrath. Be a carrier of intimate worship, praise, thanksgiving, and intimacy with Me through your steadfast love and faithfulness and grace extended, never taking offense. More and more lavish worship and freedom, love and joy that worship brings shall draw others into the light of My Love

Unfolding before you are scenic vistas of beauty and grace. Magnified before you is the purpose of your life and very being. Seek Me daily that I might lay out before you plans and areas for concern and prayer. The magnitude of all that I have for you is vast. It will take much stamina and praise, much time with Me face to face. I have strategic plans for you. Listening is the key. You must remember to just be. Be that fountain of hope and peace, love and joy springing forth from My heart. Pour forth on all alike.

Release all expectations and go forth without hesitation, releasing unto Me all residue that restricts and restrains. Monitor your progress by your joy and freedom. Be able to let go immediately all worries, fears, and false guilt. Release, release, release! Be free! All stalemates are broken. Go forth with joy, unrestricted by burdens of the mind and heart. Let today be a brand-new start. Go forth unencumbered by the past, the present, or the future. Let Me sustain you moment by moment. Let your thoughts be those of praise and thanksgiving forevermore!

Picture perfect, My love for you. Green pastures, skies of blue. Quiet pools, be not concerned. My love for you will see you through. Streams in the desert have watered your soul. They have poured forth refreshing to complete and make you whole. Seek not to conform or control. Just give forth that others might be made whole. My heart has always been, be that treasured friend. Bask in the warmth and the glow of My love, positioned in the assurance of My gifts from above. Now is the time, be not afraid. I hear and have heard every cry you have made. As you give forth all that you are and have by My hand, I bring you into My plan, complete and able to stand.

Stay close to My heart and you won't fall apart. Mistakes are made in stepping forth too soon. Make sure every detail is completely in tune. Justifying this and that is a sure and costly trap. Seek My face each day. It's the only secure way. Costly trials are averted this way, when you let Me have the final say. Stay close to My heart. Let Me be part of every thought and action proclaimed each and every day as you walk forth in My Name.

Symbols, spiritual symbols in abundance to see. When your eyes are open to see, everything you see proclaims Me. Miraculous, you say—filled with wonder each day, as the heavens proclaim the glories of the Lord. So too, the earth proclaims the same. You have heard it said, and yes you've read, such things are true. Now I show them to you. So today shall be transformed in every way as you hear and see a world that proclaims—Me. It's your destiny to see—Me!

Day 84

Singleness of mind and faith in Me has been and always is the key to a walk with Me. Struggles abound, but the sound of My voice is enough to stop the enemy of your soul in his tracks and bring forth My victory. Soundness of heart and mind come forth through a firm commitment to listening to and obeying that inner witness of My love and heart toward you. Be lifted up this day from the muck and mire that closed in on you, for My hand of blessing is upon you and forever clears the way as you come forth with praise and thanksgiving. The earth rejoices at the sound of those rejoicing in their King.

(Lord, was it a test, and did I pass?) The test was in your heart, to know that you could walk in obedience and not give into the pressure of the moment. Surgery of heart and soul takes place every time one forgoes pleasure for obedience. Once again you came to Me early to ascertain the situation from My perspective.

Peace is a tangible gift bestowed upon those who trust Me. For instance, you trust Me to speak to you with clarity and truth. This opens the door to faith, faith that I have spoken and that I can be trusted. As we walk and talk, that trust and faith become stronger and stronger. Truth becomes recognizable, and that is discernment. Let Me teach you each day.

Free fall into My arms. The forces of evil surround you for the kill, but My power is greater. Have I not said, "I have put you in a safe place surrounded by My love"? My love is a shield to you to bring you through to victory. Nothing shall stay My hand of victory in your life. I have commanded it, and it shall come forth. Go forth in faith and trust like a child with a loving, powerful Father who leads, guides, and protects saying, "This is the way, walk ye in it." Go forth with freedom, tenacity, and joy. I am with you!

My hand is upon you to bless you. My heart yearns after you that you know Me more intimately. Keep pressing in with all your heart. My way for you is blessing. Be free! Fly free! Think free! Sing free! My way for you is freedom with a song in your heart and praise and joy extolling all I have done and created. Liken it as to the days of your youth. We skipped through the fields together with few cares. Lying on your back, pondering a white cloud in a blue cloudless sky. Simple pleasures catching your attention with joy as you walked with Me with trust and love. So it is now, but with the strength and confidence of adulthood. Be strengthened this day in My Presence. Draw in My peace. My simple pleasures shall overtake you and cause you to see Me in a greater dimension.

It is a lifestyle of listening and walking, listening and talking, basking in My love and giving it forth with joy. I send you forth this day to play in My garden of life, fit and secure in My love. Many will come into this garden with you to bask in My love and play with you in My Presence, for in My Presence is fullness of joy. In this garden is every good thing for your development, enhancement, and advancement, nothing lacking. It is a garden of hope, for I place within each heart that enters, the knowledge of My love and care, and from that knowledge springs freedom. Linger in My garden each day. Let Me teach you how to play. For in My garden every action and reaction is led by My heart and sets you apart as a precious child of My heart. Through you, I can impart My heart, for you have come apart from the racing, humdrum ways of empty days into the garden of My joyful praise. Stay in this garden all of your days.

Destiny Proclaimed

Freely you have received, freely give
(Matthew 10:8).

Day 85

My treasures I have given you to love and care for; the treasures of My heart have become the treasures of your heart. I will continue to establish you in every area of your life. It has been a fight to stand strong and secure within the framework I have given you, but you have prevailed. You have left a discernable trail for others to follow with grace as they seek and follow My face. Trials come and go, but they cause you to sow precious seed along the path, that others might not lack. I have trained you along the way, raising you up to proclaim each day to all I place along your way, "I know not how, or where, or what, but this much I do know, in My God I can trust. He encircles Me with His love and leads Me gently like a dove. Among His treasures I am found and together we walk on solid ground. Our hearts are united with the bond of love which we learned from our Father above."

I open the door and draw forth from My treasure chest mighty and wonderful gifts to gladden your heart. Continue to seek My face in this place of wonderment. Trials have opened the door to more, more of My heart and gifts for you. You have sought the Giver not the gifts, and now I give you the gifts. Sup the cup of remembrance. Happiness has always been your prayer when it seemed that it was never there. The key has always been looking to Me. The times and seasons have brought you thus far, causing you to know who you are, a child of the King, complete in everything. And now My precious child, My face you shall see to set My people free. You counted the cost. I shall give you the lost and you shall set them free to be all they were created to be, by taking them to the Cross. They shall see and rejoice and shall make the choice to remain in My care, out of the enemy's lair. And together, the decision made, to repent in the day of My favor and love. The time is now, the need is great. The heart needs of My children you will not forsake. But go to the heart of the matter with clarity from above, proclaiming My constant and abiding love. First this treasured heart you'll see. Then this one you'll bring to Me to set them free. Treasures galore I bring your way, each and every day.

A life hidden in Me is paved with hopes and dreams of the unseen. It is a test to come into My rest. Precious truth gathered each day along this way. I am teaching you once again to play in My Presence each day. I've lightened the load, cleared your abode. With your focus on Me, you're beginning to see and walk in My peace with its full release. You have answered the Call, giving it your all. My will for you has always been, see the enemy and win. His tactics known, his cover blown. With lightning speed, crush each seed.

I charge you this day! Know the hearts of My people. Study them and love them for who they are. That love will loose their lives from fear and doubt. That love will set them free. Be a messenger of My love, joy, freedom, and truth. Restore their confidence through Me. Help them see their potential in Me. Be a standard of love, freedom, and joy. Every time you hug each one and smile at each one, you impart these precious elements of My heart. It is a package deal.

Day 86

My heart goes with you, My child, in everything you do. (*Lord, my heart overflows with love for You and for Your people.*) Your heart will continue to open wide to My people, exposing My heart of love for them. The love feast will grow and you will find yourself walking more and more in My Glory. Be encouraged this day. I see your heart. I have made you part of My big plan of redemption. I will hold you steady and secure in the palm of My hand and nothing shall pluck you out or cause you shame.

Seek Me, My child, with your whole heart, holding nothing back to yourself. I will give you rest in ways you know not of, for the fields are ripe for harvest and it will take strength, health, and vitality to harvest. The training has been severe to bring forth the needed results, but the victories shall be many. Strength of purpose is your strength, and My song in the night shall be your springboard to victory. Praising Me is your strength. It draws My angels to you for protection and brings sweet peace. Protection is yours, My child, to walk in My strength, My love, and My direction. Open doors are My blessing and provision. Walk through them with victory and a song in your heart. Be removed from the pressures of this world and walk in the realm of the miraculous. Sing with delight My songs of love and praise. I am with you all of your days. Feed My sheep. Snuggle My lambs. Breathe love and life into their hearts.

Settling in on you is a greater sense of your destiny. Liken it to a child who knows her daddy loves her and all He has is hers. But as she grows up, the awe of all that is set before her begins to dawn on her, the responsibility, favor, and open doors. It is all yours, My child, and the ramifications are endless. A sense of destiny and responsibility drives you. The heaviness of it shall lift and in its place shall rest the pure bubbling effervescent water of My Spirit bubbling over with joy, loosing those to respond with freedom, favor, and joy. See the darkness burst into Sonlight. See the past merge into the present with peace and favor. See My light rest upon you to accomplish all I set before you with love, favor, and joy. Slide into the passenger's seat and let Me be the driver, taking you from sea to sea with glee and freedom.

The world looks for standardized Christianity (rules and regulation). I have come to set all free. Two rules I have given. Love the Lord your God with all your mind, body, soul, and spirit; and show that love to your brothers and sisters. Stalemates are broken and lives set free in the presence of that kind of love. Seek the Giver and not the gifts, and the gifts will be yours to bestow upon My people with love.

And so you have it, My child, your destiny proclaimed, proclaiming My love your aim. Proclaiming in thought, word, and action the reality and truth of My love. It has been said that a picture is worth a thousand words. I have made your life to be a picture of My love and faithfulness. Many shall see and believe. They will know you would never deceive and so they shall see and believe and receive.

The Christian world has feared and rejected. I fear not and reject not. I give, forgive, and restore. Do as I do! Restoration is My gift to you. Would I not do for you what I expect you to minister to others? I give that you might give. Receive and give. Receive and give. It is a never-ending cycle of love.

Day 87

Filtered through My love is everything that comes into your life. Pieces of the puzzle continue to pop up before your face. Patience through the years has been the key. It has brought you to this place of grace. And now in this place which has seen much toil, comes a refreshing fragrance to aerate this soil. Fortunate to be envied are those whose hope is in the Lord. Fortunate to be envied are your comings and your goings. My song of love is upon your lips. Sing it forth with abandon.

My child. (*Yes, Lord.*) Reality and fulfillment of dreams, two ends of the spectrum, it seems. But within My heart, they are all a part of reality seen. So make way in your heart for your dreams to become a part of your everyday life to come. You'll find them on the run. You've sought the Giver, not the gift. Now it is My pleasure to give you the gift.

Saturate yourself in My words of love. Let them permeate your very being with praise and thanksgiving. My heart is within those words and draws forth My Spirit within you with My power and strength. The roar of the Lion does come forth from a heart that knows the joyful sound of the whisper of My heart and love. Buried deep within each heart is the resonating sound that can connect with joy to My love and heart. Your love will draw it forth. The words of My heart strengthen your inner being and give it rest. The more My words of love are magnified in your heart, the more they come forth with power and grace. My love shields you and protects you and brings you forth into a place of blessing and plenty. Rest in that love with singleness of heart and mind. Go forth with grace and peace forevermore.

Many times I have said, "Stalemates are broken when you come into My Presence." An ear to hear is the solution to every problem and every problem becomes no problem. Let Me extinguish every problem with the words of My mouth. Simple, straightforward answers are My way, every day. Settle the simplicity of My way into your heart each day. Listen closely each and every day.

Your ways are written in My book of life, created by My hand, formed by My love. Never reject as inadequate your ways. I simply add to them elements to enhance and delight your soul, to balance out the beauty of My creation. Each element of your being is created by My hand and a necessary part of the whole. Enjoy each facet of your being. Honor not one above the other. Reject not parts of your being, created lovingly by your Father and Creator. Be confident in the functioning of each facet of your being, for I have placed it there to create a beautiful picture, to reflect My love. Precious in My eyes are those who awake to the sound of My voice, at any age, to know that everything about them is precious in My sight, part of the reflection of My love. Seek Me to know how the different facets are to be used, that they not be abused. Seek Me to know which facets have never been used and what function they are to play. Seek Me to know which facets are overused and abused. Each facet is to be drawn together in unity to create a symphony of praise. Each life is created to be a symphony of praise all of their days.

Hearts are mended, pain ended with the warmth and flash of your smile, making it all worthwhile. Never let your smiles run dry because of a heart that cries. Let Me ease the pain and release the strain that you might walk in My peace once again. My heart for you has always been a safe haven. Don't let the days go by without coming to Me to dry your eyes and cause your heart to say, "God's peace is in my heart today."

Day 88

Straight and narrow is the path upon which you walk. Nothing shall veer you off course, for you see the safety of the pathway. The wild animals howl and try to divert you along the way, but they shall not, for you sense the danger and go on. Breakneck speed is not the way, but a steady tread will get you there with a song in your heart, a lightness of step and healthy feet. There is beauty along the trail and precious memories to make and enjoy. Be at peace, ignoring the clamor along the way. One step at a time will bring you to your goal with victory. Lay down the encumbrances that weigh you down and enjoy the pathway to and through My destiny for you. Your loving Father!

Many times you stand in the breach, unaware, as a bridge for those standing at a distance, causing them to be drawn to the light and truth of My love. Fear not to be that bridge. A bridge does not take on the characteristics of those who pass over it, but of the One who created it. Continue to look to Me, your Creator, for your truth and very being, and freely give of the love and faithfulness I have given you. Have I not told you, "You simply be, I'll do"? You be My love to My people. I'll do within My people what needs to be done. I have not told you to choose. I have simply told you to love. Let others judge, condemn, and reject as unworthy of their time and love. You simply—with faith and trust in Me to protect you—you simply love! Unafraid, unashamed, and unabashed, filled to overflowing, with My peace, love, and joy, led by My hand, proclaiming My Word. Is there anything else you need? Be released from all confusion and dread. Step by glorious step I shall lead you, protect you, uphold you, and show you the way. You will be astounded. Hold on for the ride of your life. Clear paths of My choosing are before you. Fear not the negative reports of others. You look to Me and rejoice in My provision and care. The doors will ever be open for you to walk through. My Glory shall guide you with strength of purpose and My love shall sustain you. Together we shall proclaim liberty to the captive and they shall know that I have sent you with great favor and that they can trust you.

It is a paradox. One loves deeply because the need has been so great. Another doesn't know how to love because the need has been so great. All over the world, the need is so great. Love covers a multitude of sins.

Steadfastness! My heart always comes to rest in the midst of steadfastness. I can trust those with steadfast hearts, for I know that their goals are My goals. My Presence and Glory becomes stronger and stronger in the presence of such steadfastness and single-mindedness. My child, minister such steadfastness and single-mindedness to others that they, too, might walk in My faithfulness and love, secure in My steadfastness and single-mindedness for them. There are no strings attached. I simply hold you in My heart, protected, safe, and snuggled there. Fear not for the darkness of night. Fear not for the fierceness of those who would assault you with their words, for you are Mine and My loving-kindness will overcome all obstacles in your path. You are secure and snuggled within My heart.

Day 89

Perilous times cause frustration and anxiety in the lives of those with no hope. I have set before you a course of action to bring hope and love to many on the trail of hopelessness. Continue to strengthen hearts with the freedom of love and hope. Continue to lift up weary arms with the promise of Spring within their hearts, bringing direction and fulfillment where there was disillusionment and fear. Release unto Me all weariness and weights. My heart for you has always been, walk with Me and win. And as you pass this simple premise on from heart to heart, each one will come apart to walk by My side, as My faithful Bride. Can you not see this mighty army marching forth from sea to sea, proclaiming My love and victory, walking free for all to see? March forth, child of My heart, unencumbered, flying free, following My lead.

The days and years have come and gone, but they've left within your heart My song. Let it ring within your heart. Let it heal the festering darts from trials past, bringing forth healing that will last. Within your heart the answer given to those who know not how to keep on living. Songs of hope, love, and faith, to lift their hearts and make them feel safe in their Father's arms, safe from harm.

My child, be patient and see the fulfillment of all your hopes and dreams. A dreamer dreams big and has the courage to say all he expects to see displayed. I have placed within you gigantic hopes and dreams and you have proclaimed them without fear. So carry on, dear child of My heart, and you will continue to play a part, brought forth by My very own hand, a wonderful part of My master plan. You're like the little tugboat that said, "I can!" And you will proclaim by every thought, word, and deed, every thought of My heart that fulfills the need. Strong and alert, proclaiming My Word. Having counted the cost, pursuing the lost. Bringing them to Me, helping them to see who they were created to be. So step out with pride, with Me at your side, never missing a beat as each step we complete.

Security in the world is fleeting. Security with Me lasts forever. Your heart has longed for security. Come up higher, My child. Cease from your striving and fall into My arms of love and security. You have known My heart as few do. Rest in My heart. Seek to respond to My slightest nudge. When you are resting in My arms, the slightest nudge seems strong and easily perceived. But when you are racing, even the strongest nudge can be missed. In My Presence, child, there is rest and clarity. Situations come and go, but make this your solid goal, to walk with Me in such a way as to never miss a word I say.

I will show you great and mighty things to thrill your heart and set you free. Forbearance has been your way to say, "This too will pass away." Now I have for you a new way, cushioned with the ability to just say, "No." Mighty rivers of strength shall cause you to say, "It should be done this way." And with that ability deep in your soul, it shall shine forth to complete and make you whole. Fear not repercussions. Fear not intense discussions. Just speak My words with full release and know all doubt and confusion will cease. Strong of will you have become. Now I will show you how it is done. To speak the works I've given you, so that others will know it's true. Straight and simple words that reach the heart, their truth to impart. The time is now. You've been pushing the plow. But now a stepping up is given.

Day 90

I have been the shelter from the storm in your life. Looking to Me, you have avoided strife. Now inserted in the midst of this unfailing plan, yet another way to say, "I can." For every time your heart reaches out to draw one in, considering not nor worrying about where they have been, a heart reaching out to know My love becomes unafraid to trust My love, for in your acceptance they have tasted My love. Prepare to reach out more than ever before. Let your heart be an open door. Refusing no one, My truth they'll see, knowing your love comes from Me. Fear not, nothing can cause you harm or alarm. My Spirit goes before, opening the doors, as My love through each one you pour. And know with a certainty, the enemy shall flee.

Streams in the desert have watered your soul. Streams in the desert have made you whole. Proclaiming forever, My heart you have found. Propelling you upward to higher ground. And now through the tempest and storms you have come. Proclaiming, "My God loves you," we are now one. Secure in My love you have become. My heart is your heart, the prize you have won. Continue proclaiming My love, it is true. Continue proclaiming, "My God does love you." Let the words of your mouth reflect the love in your heart, that others might rejoice at being a part of a life filled with peace, knowing joy and full release from the everyday trials. Frustration shall cease as they look to Me, the source of their peace, to bring contentment and full release.

My child. (*Yes, Lord.*) Linger with Me for a while. Let Me fill your cup to overflowing with My Word and with My life. Abundance is yours in all areas. Look around you. See My hand in every area of your life. I have seen your need and each need is met. Consider each area as a gift from Me. My heart is your heart and shall continue to trigger faith and strength in others. Struggle has brought it forth. Be prepared to seek Me even more as the days go by.

The fields are ripe for harvest and I am sending you forth, for My heart has become your heart for My people. Treasures they shall be to you, each one, and My light and My Glory shall shine from you and draw them in like moths to the flame. And you shall not burn them but warm them with My Word and My love. Far off in the distance you can hear the sound of tramping feet, the feet of the righteous, marching to the rhythm of My heart of love, focusing on My vision and calling, sharing a common goal, bringing forth My love to a lost and dying world.

Sound forth the rallying cry. Call forth the troops. Muster them forth to proclaim My favor and propensity for action. Now is the time. Great is My faithfulness. Masterfully I shall mold them together as one in action. Sound forth the call. My anointing is upon you to ignite their hearts and souls.

So shall it be!

Amen.

About the Author

Rosalie Willis Storment has authored four books including, *A Walk With Jesus, The Singing Bride, When God Speaks To My Heart* and *Walking on With Jesus.* She copyrighted the music to all 150 Psalms—word for word. It takes about twelve hours for her to sing them straight through. The first CD has been produced in Nashville, Tennessee, and is titled *The Psalms*, which includes twelve Psalms. The CD is available through Praise Publishing.

Rosalie is the founder and director of A Company of Women International, established in 1996. This ministry is a network of worldwide "Heart Friends" whom God has called to take His love to the nations. The same can be said of A Company of Men and A Company of Youth around the world who have come alongside A Company of Women, each loving and encouraging one another to be all they can be in Christ to fulfill their God-given destinies in Him. An important part of A Company of Women is "PraiseNet," an international prayer network through which all can pray together to meet needs and rejoice in shared victories, while connecting hearts worldwide.

Rosalie Willis Storment
P.O. Box 324
Post Falls, ID 83877-0324

E-mail: rosalieacw@gmail.com
Website: www.rosaliewillis.com
Website: www.acompanyofwomen.org
Praise Publishing: 208-773-8411

PraiseNet International Prayer E-mail Network:
praisenet@acompanyofwomen.org

Additional copies of this book and other book titles from DESTINY IMAGE™ EUROPE are available at your local bookstore.

We are adding new titles every month!

To view our complete catalog online, visit us at:
www.eurodestinyimage.com

Send a request for a catalog to:

Via Acquacorrente, 6
65123 - Pescara - ITALY
Tel. +39 085 4716623 - Fax +39 085 9431270

"Changing the world, one book at a time."

Are you an author?

Do you have a "today" God-given message?

CONTACT US

We will be happy to review your manuscript for the possibility of publication:

publisher@eurodestinyimage.com
http://www.eurodestinyimage.com/pages/AuthorsAppForm.htm